Psychic Protection

Psychic Protection

Bill Duvendack

Megalithica Books

Stafford England

Psychic Protection by Bill Duvendack
© 2019 First edition

All rights reserved, including the right to reproduce this book, or portions thereof, in any form.

The rights of Bill Duvendack to be identified as the author of this work have been asserted by him in accordance with the Copyright, Designs and Patents Act, 1988.

Editor: Storm Constantine
Layout: Storm Constantine
Cover Design: Danielle Lainton

ISBN: 978-1-912241-14-9
MB0206

Set in Book Antiqua

A Megalithica Books Publication
An imprint of Immanion Press
info@immanion-press.com
www.immanion-press.com

Contents

Protecting Yourself: A Foreword by Storm Constantine   7
Introduction   10

Section One-Physical Plane Tools
Chapter One: Proactive Health and Self-Defense   15
Chapter Two: Psychic Attacks, the Experience   34
Chapter Three: Semiprecious Stones   38
Chapter Four: A Protection Apothecary   56

Section Two-Emotional Plane Tools
Chapter Five: Emotional Health and Protection   75
Chapter Six: Vampires   93

Section Three-Mental Plane Tools
Chapter Seven: Body Language & Hypnosis   109
Chapter: Eight: Critical Thinking Tips   124

Section Four-Spiritual Tools
Chapter Nine: Daily Spiritual Regimen   141
Chapter Ten: Living Spirituality   158

Afterword   175
Bibliography for Further Reading   177
About the Author   178
Other Books by Bill Duvendack   179

Dedication

This book is dedicated to all those who want to further their self-empowerment through self-control and knowledge, rather than control of others.

Protecting Yourself
A Foreword by Storm Constantine

The philosophical principle known as Occam's Razor tells us that the simplest explanation for something is usually the correct one. Bill Duvendack keeps this principle in mind throughout the book you hold in your hands.

Psychic attack is traditionally regarded as a situation in which someone believes another person is trying to do them harm – but in secret via mind and will rather than through a physical assault, or by causing trouble with lies and accusations behind a victim's back. In this book, Bill argues that what might seem to be psychic attack could easily be the result of a host of other, simpler causes. He examines the ways in which you can protect yourself psychically – not just from potential ill-doers but from unwise life choices and habits. If you think you're under psychic attack, the chances are you're not, so it's vital to eliminate all other causes of symptoms and effects before tackling the idea that you really do have an enemy out there pitting their will against yours.

The way you look after your body is of vital importance. Being dehydrated can cause depression and anxiety, perhaps leading to the feeling that someone is working against you. An unhealthy diet, heavy on junk food, causes illness in the body, such as diabetes, which itself leads to feeling enervated and dizzy, as if someone is directing negative energy at you. Not getting enough sleep or worrying too much – all of these can contribute to a situation where you might feel weak, exhausted, disempowered and besieged. The book covers in detail how best to take care of yourself in these respects. As well as working to be physically and mentally well, you can learn how to protect yourself physically, by learning some form of self-defense; this contributes to greater well-being as you are inexorably led to feeling more in control of your life and less under threat. But once all the possible causes of physical and mental illness have been examined and dismissed, and the signs of attack are still there, it's time to consider taking action on another level.

This book gives comprehensive advice on using gem stones and herbs to protect yourself, describing in detail the properties of these materials, how they work and why they are useful. Sometimes, it might be necessary to deal with others who are causing harm – whether intentionally or in ignorance. You might've come across the 'psychic vampire' type who can drain your energy if you spend too much time in their company. You'll find descriptions of the different types of 'vampire' – not those of legend who feast on blood, but those who gorge themselves on the energy and emotions of others. Some might do so intentionally – others without realising the effect they have on people. You can develop techniques to deal with all types, preventing them from affecting you detrimentally.

The way you carry yourself also contributes to your personal psychic protection. You'll learn how to adapt your body language to help create effective armor when dealing with day to day situations, when someone might seek to bully, control or subdue you. There are tips on how to think critically, analysing situations to get the best results. Overall, with practical techniques in addition to those I've described here, *Psychic Protection* provides tools to deal with the ups and downs of work, socialising and the home, so that you may become the commander of your life rather than a victim, blown this way and that, feeling out of control. This is an empowering book. No matter how experienced you are in the subject of psychic protection there will be ideas and suggestions here to add to your store of knowledge.

Introduction

You may be asking yourself "Why *another* book on psychic protection? Hasn't this topic been discussed to death?" Yes, it has, in books both good and bad. There are a few things that separate this book from the countless others that already exist. First, the emphasis is on practicality. You will find discussions here on helpful herbs and semiprecious gemstones that are useful. However, you will also find information on reading body language, and techniques you can use when you might not have other tools available. The layout of this book is also unique in that we will look at tools and techniques associated with the four planes in the Western Esoteric Tradition. This point alone means you can flip quickly to the appropriate section for speedy research. Tools for the physical, emotional, mental, and spiritual planes will be discussed in depth. After all, a large part of success involves using the right tool for the job.

Special attention will also be given to discernment. Not every hardship, challenge, or lesson we go through while we are incarnated is a psychic attack, after all! As a matter of fact, something I learned a long time ago is that if you think you are being psychically attacked, you are most likely not. To understand this takes an education in astrology and karma, and thus both of those points will be addressed in here, albeit cursorily, but enough to establish a baseline for critical thinking. This does set the stage for a warning, though, which is that if you are disempowered, guilty of Chicken Little syndrome, then you will either find yourself challenged to get through this, or you may not resonate with it at all. (Chicken Little syndrome is when you constantly think the sky is falling. In other words, constantly worrying that situations will go bad. By worrying in this way, you can create a negative event to happen in the future.) Many people would rather play the victim than put in the hard work necessary for growth, and this book is not for them.

Like my earlier title *Spirit Relations*, this book is a manual intended for those who want to do the work necessary to protect themselves in everyday life. Because of this, spiritual fantasy vs spiritual reality will also be discussed in here. In this way, this book will challenge what you think you know, and while it will elucidate subjects in clear, concise, and practical terms, it will also encourage you to question what happens to you in day-to-day life from a new empowered perspective. When you have finished reading it and implementing what is discussed, you will find your life is more under your control than ever before. I have worked with every technique in these pages and most of them extensively at that, so I can say from experience that these are proven techniques that should be available to all. If you are an experienced Will worker, you can enjoy what is contained herein because of the wide-ranging topics and subjects discussed. And if you are a beginner, this material can help you avoid a lot of issues that many in the past have suffered, as they performed trial and error with their lives as petri dishes. Enjoy, and be ready to step outside your comfort zone. This is the only way growth occurs, though. Don't believe me? Ask any seed that has broken the comfort zone of soil through conflict to become a fully blossoming plant.

Cheers!

Bill Duvendack
St Louis MO USA
Spring Equinox 2019

Section One
Physical Plane Tools

Chapter One
Proactive Health and Self-Defense

Physical Health

Let's start with a disclaimer. I am not a dietician, nor a doctor of any variety, so take what I say here as inspiration and additional information to what your health care professional says. The material in this chapter and the next are meant as additional perspectives and insights into physical and mental health and the professionals that address such topics. This is not meant as replacement information. In other words, don't be an idiot. Are we good? If so, let's go.

There are many people in the world who have health situations they deal with on a regular basis. Some of these are visible while others are invisible, and it is not the place of this book to make any judgments or comparisons on said people or topics. After all, to quote the World Teacher Aleister Crowley, "It is the mark of the mind untrained to take its own processes as valid for all men, and its own judgments for absolute truth." Just because you or I can do something doesn't mean everyone can do it, and this is an important fact to keep in mind while reading this chapter.

Some authors in this field will tell you to get healthy, but they fail to define what that means. Or, worse yet, they will tell you what it means, leaving out the fact that this is from their experience and perspective only, and may not apply to everyone who reads their book. I completely agree with them it is wise to get healthy, but that means health as it relates to you, not necessarily me, nor really anyone else. In order to do this, you should consult with a health care professional to get a handle on your health. Perusing topics on your own is inadequate. Arrange a consultation with a health care professional to establish a baseline and then peruse said topics. The point of this is not to become the picture of health you find in pulp fitness and beauty magazines. Rather, the point of this is to make sure you have a firm grasp on your health so that you are more empowered in your life and are in a better position to read the messages from your body and the universe.

For example, let's say you have undiagnosed diabetes. This may manifest as feelings of vertigo or lack of energy, among other characteristics, and you may interpret this to be a psychic attack, when in reality it is your health calling for attention and has nothing to do with a psychic attack. A large part of dealing with psychic protection lies in the critical thinking tool of Occam's Razor. In short, Occam's Razor simply says that most times in life, the simplest answer and solution are generally the correct ones. Competent ghost hunters are very familiar with this when they explore a location. Instead of assuming everything is a spirit, they will look for copper wires and other explanations before jumping to conclusions. This is the application of logic at its finest. Claiming a phenomenon has a supernatural origin should be a last resort conclusion rather than a first option. The best way to get into this headspace is to have a firm grasp and understanding of where your health is currently at. To come back to the previous example, if you know you have diabetes and you experience those symptoms, then you will know what you are experiencing is related to it and not some supernatural cause.

An extension of this is to learn how to read your body. This is a little more challenging and may require more effort than just setting up a consultation with a health care professional. Did you know that one of the manifestations of dehydration is depression? It is true. Sometimes when we are depressed, we are really just lacking the appropriate amount of water our body requires to perform at optimal levels. Thus, the next time you feel yourself depressed, drink a decent amount of water for a while and see how you feel in time. One of the ways you can tell if you are dehydrated is to look at your urine in the toilet. If it is a dark color, chances are that you are dehydrated. This paragraph is only one example of a lot of material that is available for those who are willing to do the research, and you can see how valuable it is to know these things. Sometimes people are depressed, and they think there is a supernatural cause for it, when in reality it is the result of biological and physical needs connected with their body.

Another example is cramps. No, I am not talking about menstrual cramps. I am a guy after all, so really I don't have any right nor place to discuss such things. I am talking about experiencing cramps in your legs or hands. Cramps can often make situations like sleep paralysis occur. Many times, this can indicate a deficiency in potassium. This can get into sticky territory though, because of a topic often times misunderstood, which is sleep paralysis. Sleep paralysis is actually perfectly natural, but what makes it distinctive is that sometimes people wake up during it, generally having horrific nightmares in the process, and many of those times people think they are under psychic attack from creatures from another world, which of course they are not. An entire book could be written about the subject, specifically from an occult perspective, so I will not spend a lot of time on it here, other than to show how it relates to psychic protection. If you know about sleep paralysis, then you can more accurately discern whether you are suffering from that or an actual psychic attack. Logically, and more frequently, someone suffers sleep paralysis rather than an attack from a nonphysical entity. Sleep paralysis basically occurs when your body becomes immovable in order to protect you while you are asleep. It does this so you don't do something that would be damaging to yourself while you are resting. As you can see, a potassium deficiency could cause more severe sleep paralysis due to the cramping factor. We can get cramps at any time though, and if we don't know about the potassium link, we may think it is the result of an attack.

Mental Health

So far we have been discussing physical symptoms and health, but let's take a moment to discuss mental health. I put this section here instead of the mental plane chapter of the book because many times mental health is due to a chemical imbalance or some sort of physical defect rather than a state of mind. We will discuss traumas in the next chapter where we focus on emotional health. Mental health is as serious if not more so than physical health, and so it deserves some time and attention here, especially in light of a lot of misconceptions, dogmatic views, and outright incorrect information that is currently popular in the world.

I want to start off addressing a common phrase currently in use that gets a bad reputation, but that is due to being taken out of context and being misunderstood: "I meditate, not medicate." I first learned this phrase at the turn of the century when I was just getting integrated with the local neo-pagan community, and I first heard it from several ex or current hippies. And yes, when I say hippies here, I am specifically referring to those from the 1960s and 1970s, and not this new form of hippy that I see out and about in today's world. Yes, there are many differences, but that is a conversation for another time and place.

The point and context of this saying that people tend to ignore or are simply ignorant of is that it came about from the generation that furthered the exposure of many drugs into society in an attempt to open minds and increase the spiritual progress of the species, especially in the Western world. The phrase really has a two-fold meaning. First, it is saying that many use drugs for spiritual progress, when meditation works just as well, if not better. Secondly, it is saying that sometimes people use prescription drugs as crutches, choosing not to face whatever it is the drug addresses, and this practice is wrong and unhealthy. However, remember that this phrase is quite old now, and its transmission has been diluted by newer generations that only heard it, but have never heard it explained like this. I was fortunate enough to have it explained to me. In current society, people use this phrase as an attack on the pharmaceutical industry and indirectly people who use artificial substances instead of natural cures. Which of course means they miss the whole point of what it is really saying. You can't blame them for missing the point, though. Their heart is in the right place in that they are saying it is better to use natural means than live with a crutch or in denial, and in these times of expensive pharmaceutical drugs that have the side effect of "may cause death," there is truth in what they say.

But, the major problem with this is that people use it as a blanket term and do not apply critical thinking to its application. Of course, it is always wiser to meditate than medicate. There are several things to consider before making a decision about this, though. First, psychedelics and many other drugs are fantastic gateways to further spiritual growth and personal gnosis, so using them in the beginning of your spiritual journey is not necessarily wrong, and anyone who tells you otherwise has no understanding of shamanism or the roots of current humanity. However, if one never progresses beyond their use, then they become crutches and thus limit true growth. Secondly, many people cannot meditate instead of medicate, because the medications they are on balance out chemical imbalances in the brain, so the pharmaceuticals are acting in the stead of what natural chemicals would be doing, if they were present in proper and healthy amounts. Third, why is the phrase an either or statement at all? I know many people who are on pharmaceutical drugs to balance out brain chemistry who still meditate, so why pressure someone into something unhealthy, like being guilted into meditating and not medicating? Yes, it is true that guilt is a choice though, so that should be considered as well.

Another problem with the phrase is that a strong argument is being made that the modern psychiatry movement, including the over prescription of pharmaceuticals, is retarding the spiritual evolution of the species, and is therefore detrimental en masse. Many of the great religions and spiritual practices of the world have their roots in spiritual experiences triggered by natural mind-altering substances and possibly even mental illnesses. One example of this is that it is widely believed the *Book of Revelation* in the Judeo-Christian *Bible* was written by St John while he was on a hallucinogenic journey! Another, more controversial example of this, is that many of the times key spiritual leaders and influencers through history claim to have heard stories, they may have been suffering from split personalities, hearing voices in their heads, rather than actually interacting with spirits. This one point alone could be discussed in depth in a separate volume to this book, but it does illustrate the point that many times throughout history mental issues and altered states of consciousness have actually bettered us as a species rather than retarded our growth. In the modern world, pharmaceuticals are dulling and oftentimes stopping our spiritual experiences, which as you can see when you look at the world, is hurting our development.

Am I advocating for or against using mind altering

Psychic Protection

substances with regards to spiritual practices? Those who truly know me already know the answer to that, but in short, it comes down to *Do what thou wilt shall be the whole of the law*. Make the decision that is best and most appropriate for you, but before you decide, DO YOUR RESEARCH!

Dr Israel Regardie is famously known for making the statement that before you begin magick you should get a clean bill of health from a mental health professional (I am paraphrasing his exact words by the way). This makes sure you are mentally competent, and it helps to establish a baseline for collating the results of your work. However, later in life he changed his view on this for various reasons. Ultimately, this concept is something it is wise to ponder, but there is no dogmatic right or wrong as to whether or not you should do it. The choice is yours. His idea of establishing a mental baseline is a good idea and logically sound, though, which means it is worth considering before you begin. If you are already working with magick, then it is wise to periodically review your journals to see how much you've changed through your experiences.

All of this should be kept in mind when considering psychic protection, because it is wise to know what something is going to do to your body before you ingest it. It is also wise to know what your limitations are, and to accept them. For example, if you are schizophrenic and choose not to take medicine for it, then how can anything you spiritually experience be good? Yes, I did mention above that sometimes these things have helped the evolution of the species, but that was then and this is now. It is a different world we live in, and because of that, the responsibility is upon us to look at things differently and from a more enlightened perspective. Before you decide you are under a psychic attack, make sure your mental health is in order. If it is not, then you're probably not under psychic attack, but rather your mental condition is manifesting, and thus not the fault of anyone else. Then again, everything is your fault if you're any good.

One final piece of the health picture to consider has been advanced by metaphysics over the last few decades and is based on a magical principle. This is the idea that parts of the body, and corresponding conditions, can be interpreted symbolically and can reveal nonphysical situations we should address for our own health and growth. This idea gets a lot of criticism, though, for the same reason as I mentioned earlier: it is commonly misunderstood or misapplied. The theory behind this is that the human body is the microcosm of the macrocosm of the greater multiverse we inhabit, and thus is based on the Hermetic axiom, "As above, so below." Thus, the working model is that if we are experiencing something physically wrong with a part of our body, it is telling us about a deeper spiritual wound that is calling for our attention. An extension of this states that when we address the spiritual situation, the physical body will heal. At this point it should be clear why this receives criticism. Here again, people take this too literally and as an absolute when it is not. I have found it to be very profound and of great use through the years, though, and it is important enough to discuss here. Yes, you can use your body this way to reveal deeper spiritual, mental, and emotional situations that are calling for attention. However, and this is a large caveat, there are a few other factors that should be taken into account: genetic karma, spiritual karma, the randomness of living in a world where free will is the rule, and family karma. Keeping those points in mind alone can prevent one from looking at the matter from a mutually exclusive and absolute perspective. After all, everything is life is a sliding scale of grey.

Here is an example to illustrate the point. Let us say you are currently stuck on a spiritual quandary. Then, seemingly out of the blue, your left eye becomes red with irritation, and you begin scratching it. If you are right-handed, the message here is that there is something not being seen that has to do with your emotions and/or intuition. If you are left-handed, though, it could mean there is something logical you are not seeing. In either case, the message is that something is calling for your attention, and when you address it, you can move forward. Why does your dominant hand matter, you ask? Well, most of the symbolism discussed here, and its metaphysical roots, are based on the world of a right-hander, which means the foundation is outdated and toxic. True, most people are right-handed, but there are a large number of people who are not, and if you don't account for this, the esoteric meaning and teaching behind this translation of symbolism will always be slanted against left-handers. In most sources, the right side of the body corresponds to the mental plane and the left side corresponds to the emotional, but if you are left-handed, this means the insight from that material will always be against you. I know this because I am left-handed, and many years ago got sick and tired of living in a world that was bigoted against me. I had to seek out better teachers and information to explain this. Eventually I found it, and it became the basis for what I am sharing here. Interpret this material from the perspective of dominant hand vs non-dominant hand, rather than right or left. Consider the fact that when metaphysics was just coming into being, the church considered left-handed people evil or sinister, which means we really can't trust the justification for this interpretation. It is better to say the dominant side corresponds to the mental plane messages, and the non-dominant corresponds to the intuitive. This can be a useful interpretation technique to use, but don't forget to factor in the various types of karma I mentioned above. Sometimes what you are dealing with has nothing to do with spiritual growth in the sense of how I'm discussing it here.

Sometimes you might be dealing physically with karma connected to lessons being learned and situations being worked through during this incarnation.

Let's look at an example. Say that you are right-handed and you broke your right wrist. Using the above information, you could deduce that maybe you are not being flexible enough with your thinking. Or, it could simply be that you made a poor decision. This is another example of Occam's Razor in action. Sometimes the spiritual lesson is something so obvious we tend to miss it, looking for deeper meaning when there is none. Keeping this in mind when looking for psychic attacks is very powerful, for it reminds us just how much of our lives, and what occurs in it, are under our control. We should always look at ourselves first and foremost before searching for external causes. After all, a major spiritual teaching that has been around for a long time is that every interaction we have is an interaction with the divine in some way, shape, or form. But if we are divinity incarnate, then that interaction is often time with ourselves.

Diet

Here again I reiterate the disclaimer at the beginning of the chapter. For accurate personal insight into diet, please consult a professional. Having said that, let us proceed. A proper diet is necessary not just for good health, but also as a defense against psychic attack. If your diet is in accord with what you need for your health, you are in a healthy state of mind to see what might be a psychic attack and what is the result of poor diet choices. One parable of wisdom to remember is that garbage in does equal garbage out. Many times, I have seen someone with a poor diet think they are being psychically attacked when in reality, it is the consequences of their poor dietary choices catching up with them. For example, if you eat low quality food and it gives you diarrhea, that does not mean you are the target of some cacodemon, but rather your body is protesting what you are doing to it.

A lot of emphasis has been placed on the diet from a spiritual perspective over the last few decades, and while a lot of this emphasis has been good, some of it has been toxic to the point of physically damaging, and thus works against any spiritual growth you may otherwise be achieving. Fad diets and health trends are also best avoided whenever possible. Yes, there is wisdom in keeping up with information and the ideas connected with this, but to simply jump on a bandwagon for the sake of being trendy is always toxic. By eating what is best for you and adhering to a diet that optimizes your health to the best of your abilities, you increase your body's protection not only to disease and breakdown, but also to misinterpreting signs of psychic attack. Really though, if we're going to discuss diet, we should break it down into two components: physical and liquid.

The human body is roughly 75% water. What this means on a practical level is that we should consume a lot of water on a daily basis just to maintain good health. Drinking fluids simply isn't enough. We should specifically drink a lot of water. Yes, juices and other liquids that are good for the body should definitely be indulged in, but water should be considered the baseline and standard. In the past, information has come out that says you should drink 'X' amount of water to be healthy, but here again, there is a major problem with that, in that not everybody has the same weight or physical build, so how can water consumption for everyone be the same, and set in stone? That's just illogical. I will not get into specifics here with how much water people of different weights and body builds should ingest because it is not my place. Rather, I simply want to emphasize that this should be researched, and the amount of water you drink should be in line with what is best for your body. Earlier, I mentioned that one of the symptoms of dehydration is depression, and it is worth reiterating here. If you are depressed, drink water. If you think some sort of supernatural force is the cause of your depression, drink water first to make sure that is not the case. It is not enough to simply *think* you have enough water in your system when you are assessing psychic assault. There are many causes for dehydration after all. We lose water not just from sweat, but also from different environmental factors, too. For example, it is easy to become dehydrated during cold seasons because the air is dry, and therefore we need more water to maintain standard hydration. This was a difficult lesson for me to learn, but here is how I learned it. I first observed that during cold weather I had a tendency to get depressed easier. At first, I thought it was seasonal affective disorder, but then I learned how the body gets dehydrated easier in cold conditions, so I increased my water intake as an experiment to see if it affected my moods, and guess what? The more I increased my water consumption, the less depressed I was! Since then, I am very mindful of my water intake during periods of cold, and my emotional control has vastly improved. I also frequently check my urine as mentioned above, whether I am feeling emotionally out of sorts or not, just to be safe. I would rather err on the side of caution, after all, than get blindsided. If you are dehydrated, your urine will be a darker color than normal. The trick is to avoid becoming paranoid about it!

When it comes to food, it is another story. First, do your research and consult your professional. I will avoid having a detailed discussion about this for that reason, but there are some key points I do want to address. Some of them are physical, and some are metaphysical, but all should be kept in mind. Eating a healthy and balanced diet in line with your physical body is the best way to maintain health. Some people say being vegetarian is best for your spiritual growth, while some people say being vegan is best, but both of those views are junk spirituality. There is no "best diet for spiritual growth." That is an illusion at best, and an attack on your health by pretentious people at worst. As with most situations in life though, especially those we've been discussing here, it all has to do with what is best for your body, nothing more, nothing less. I know many people who would love to eat meat, but they can't because their bodies can't handle it. Conversely, I know many people that would love to avoid meat, but they can't because their bodies can't handle it. You could also apply this logic to veganism, too, and it still holds true. While some people simply want to avoid eating animals, that is a conversation for another time and place.

The main take away lesson from this is to know what is best for your body, and to respond accordingly, regardless of what anyone says you *should* do. Unless they are a certified health care professional, they don't know, and are simply reiterating what they were taught, told, or what works best for them. The key to working with this is to remember "everything in moderation, including moderation." This phrase should be tempered with a strong warning though, which is that sometimes if you stray from your diet, you may end up more damaged, beyond repair, or even dead, which means that a lot of times your necessary diet for health does not give you room to stray, a point which should be taken into consideration very seriously. But I like to employ the 80/20 rule. This is an approach that effectively says, "For eighty percent of the time I am on the straight and narrow, but I allow myself to cheat twenty percent of the time."

Supplements are worth mentioning here as well, but only in passing. Sometimes a busy lifestyle means it is nigh on impossible to eat healthily at every mealtime, and many people consider taking supplements to compensate nutrients when they might otherwise be lacking. For approximately a decade I worked anywhere from two to three jobs, seven days a week, averaging ten to twelve hours each day, and because of that I relied heavily on supplements, so I know the feeling. However, I ceased that when my schedule and lifestyle changed. Getting nutrients from food is always better than getting them from supplements, but sometimes it can't be helped. Before taking any supplements, consult the appropriate professional to help you with your choices.

There is also a metaphysical side to your diet and that has to do with the colors of the foods you eat. One food theory is that you can eat foods of a particular color to produce a particular effect. For example, if you want more optimism in your life, eat yellow foods. Often times, this theory is extended to address the chakras and their colors. Another example: If you want to improve your ability to work with the throat chakra, eat blue foods. I understand the logic here, but as I am pretty sure you can see, this is something that should be handled very carefully, for the health considerations mentioned above. Yes, this can be useful to increase mindfulness, but not if it is detrimental to one's overall health.

Food as it serves in magical functions is something else entirely though, so let us take a moment to address it. An age-old magical teaching states that one should not eat anything heavy before executing magical rituals because it will ground the individual and higher states of consciousness may not be achieved. I have seen this to be true time and again. This should be tempered with the diet as discussed above though, and there are a few other important points to address. The standard magical teaching is that one should not eat for a period of three hours before ritual. The teaching is that this helps mentally prepare the person and the body for the incoming energies. However, as you now know, if that is not possible for you to do for health reasons, then don't attempt it. It is better to be safe than sorry. Often people will eat a light snack before ritual as a substitute. I don't want to get into a diatribe of eating for ritual, as this is not the place, but the other important piece of the puzzle is that eating something heavy after ritual serves to ground you back into your body, and this is very important indeed, especially if you are attending a ritual that is not at your home. Being grounded and focused after ritual is good because it brings your attention back to the physical world, and when driving a vehicle this is a safety measure as much as it is anything else.

The way this applies to psychic protection is that if you do not ground after ritual you open yourself to the possibility of psychic attack by not fully extracting yourself from the ritual. Rituals need time to work, and the separation of consciousness after a ritual helps to ensure the results come at a time that is best in line with your greatest growth and good and not potentially hazardous, which would be the case if you drive home while ungrounded.

Finally, the last point of health to address in this chapter is that of a healthy sleep schedule. I cannot stress this enough for various reasons, and this is as important to pay attention to as the physical food we consume and the water we drink. According to professionals, at least last time I checked, a healthy amount of sleep is somewhere between 5-8 hours a night. Anything less than that is not enough, and anything more than that is too much. Our bodies rest during sleep. Our mind gets a chance to process events. Advanced magick practitioners even do a lot of magical work during this time.

Lack of sleep, or an unhealthy sleep schedule, can put you in a vulnerable mental state, susceptible to psychic attack, but also to tricks of the mind that may make you think you are under attack, when in reality it is your mind calling for attention because it is sick. The body is naturally attuned to sleeping at night, but for many this is not a possibility. Lack of sleep can also open the door to mental disorders if it occurs for an extended period of time. Many books have been written on the subject and there exists an entire set of sleep professionals to assist you with this if it is an issue. But I mention it here because before you assume you are being psychically attacked, make sure your sleep is healthy and that it is not the symptom of a sick mind, or one that is in some other way negatively affected by sleep issues. This also means that if you are having sleep issues, it may be wise to skip any sort of formal ritual work until they are resolved, as your perceptions of the results of your ritual may be skewed.

It may not seem like this chapter has much to do with psychic protection, and while I have given several examples throughout, you may still be left wondering why I started this book with this material. Bluntly, it was inspired by a teaching from the "Builders of the Adytum" (BOTA) mystery school. In the beginning of the program they tell you that before you begin their work (which could be extrapolated out here to be THE Work), you should have your house in order. In their context they are not talking about your physical home, but rather your physical world life. Before pursuing psychic protection methods, make sure you are centered, focused, and grounded, and that is the point of this chapter. Often, we think we are a target when in reality it is our own irresponsibilities that are coming back to bite us in the ass, as the saying goes. By being proactive about the ideas discussed here, you put yourself on solid ground to move forward in a more self-empowered way.

Self-Defense

Most books about psychic protection don't even touch on this topic, and I am still at a loss as to why. Bluntly, learning

Psychic Protection

a form of self-defense should be a given, but since this is neglected frequently, we will examine it here. This is one of the most if not *the* most powerful form of psychic protection because it is a protection tool for the physical world we live in, and therefore should be foundational. However, understanding it and working with it are a little more complex than one can imagine, so let's get started.

As a precursor to this is exercise, (and which we touched on this earlier in the chapter), I simply want to call your attention to it now to pave the way for what follows. Self-defense takes many different forms, so rather than go into detailed conversations about all of them, I will give highlights and principles and will trust you will seek to learn what appeals to you. Part of addressing self-defense is in knowing your limits and interests. Not everyone is a picture of health, and therefore some of the classic self-defense techniques such as Karate, Jeet Kune Do, or Ju Jitsu, may not work in particular situations. If this is the case, then find some other way to defend yourself. The best way though, is through discrimination. Knowing how and what situations to avoid are of the utmost importance for protecting yourself. This doesn't always work, as we know, and when it doesn't, other means should be employed. I strongly suggest learning a form of martial art, but this is a wide-ranging category, so it is highly subjective to you, your path, and your health. While many don't realize it, Tai Chi is a form of martial art, and I list it here to show that not all such arts are as aggressive as stereotypes and propaganda may lead us to believe. In any case, if you are interested in pursuing this direction, I encourage you to do your research and experiment to see what works best for you. Let's play devil's advocate though, and say that because of health problems and challenges, none of them work for you. If that is the case, then there are alternative ways to consider.

The most common forms of self-defense outside of

martial arts involve tools and weapons. While this may make many uncomfortable, the alternative should be even more uncomfortable, the alternative being a life lived in fear. After all, fear is failure, as the good book says. Some of the most common tools people use for defense include pepper spray and tasers. While I advocate people practicing self-defense, I also understand that as we change our focus to discuss tools and weapons, another perspective should be considered, and that is mental health. We touched on this broadly earlier, but let's face facts. Some people are not mentally balanced enough to be trusted with any of these weapons. This imbalance could be caused by unhealed trauma, or power going to their head, inflating and distorting the ego. Just because you have these tools and weapons at your disposal doesn't mean you should use them liberally or frequently. Conversely, if you find you are using them more often than not, then it is time to look in the mirror and see what you're doing wrong in your life to continually find yourself in positions where you have to use them. If learning a martial art is not for you, then perhaps carrying pepper spray or a taser will work just fine.

If these don't work either though, there is another route to go: weapons. Straight up weapons should be considered as a form of protection, and I cannot stress contemplating these enough. I'm not saying everyone should have one, but too many people dismiss this because they would rather rely on herbs, stones, or oils, but I can tell you from firsthand experience those don't do any good in certain situations. As an Islamic proverb says, "Trust in Allah, but tie up your camel." Carrying a knife or being trained in the use of a gun cannot be understated. Do I believe everyone should do this? Of course not, but this should be considered none the less. Yes, these are not possibilities in some countries of the planet, or in some facilities you may frequent, but they should still be considered none the less.

By not thinking about them, you are neglecting looking at a comprehensive picture of what self-defense is, what it means, and how to do it.

This may seem like an odd discussion to have in this book, but remember that if you can't protect yourself on the physical plane, you really don't have much of a platform to work from when it comes to working with the higher and finer planes. This is true of many metaphysical topics and not just self-defense ones, by the way. In some ways it is the karmic law of attraction, and in others it is just good, old fashioned, spell work and logic.

The main difference between learning a system of martial arts for self-defense and using a weapon or a tool is that if you work with martial arts, you are training yourself to be the weapon. You are also creating muscle memory so well that you can subconsciously fall into that behavior when necessary. A tool or a weapon takes conscious use, but a martial art kicks in automatically if the situation merits it. Martial arts also create mental discipline and strength, both of which can assist you very well in other areas of your life, especially when it comes to rituals and living your spiritual path. In all of these cases, trust your judgment and seek out trained professionals to learn from.

Chapter Two
Psychic Attacks, the Experience

In order to understand protection, you should first understand the attack. Being psychically attacked is quite an interesting experience to say the least, and varies from person to person, based on individual empathy, interaction with the general public, people to people skills, and individual psychic abilities. What one sensitive person would call a psychic attack is not necessarily what another would recognize as a psychic attack, or even go so far as to call one. Psychic attacks occur when negative and/or lower vibrational energy is directed your way. This energy is more direct and focused than higher vibrational energies, so it hits a very visceral and gut level. (If you are already familiar with what a psychic attack feels like, feel free to skip this chapter, unless you want a refresher and a different perspective.) Let's clarify what I mean by lower and vibrational energies, too, before proceeding.

This is discussed throughout the book, but it does necessitate a brief mention here. I will use practical terms and examples, just to clarify. Lower vibrations are things that are denser and more finite in a lot of ways. I say "things" here, because everything is vibrating at a different rate. For example, steel vibrates at a much lower rate than glass, and glass at a much higher rate than plastic. This idea is also true when it comes to beliefs, principles, and behaviors. Love is a higher, sometimes more fragile, vibration than hate. This idea is reflected in the phrase "you get farther with honey than you do with vinegar." Higher vibrations are very uplifting, whether they are inspirations for your creativity, or emotions such as love.

But they are also more fragile because of this. A feeling associated with psychic attacks is an almost palpable feeling of energy, usually, but not always, through emotions. Results can also manifest in the form of headaches, nausea, instinctive feelings, and even more physical ways.

Thus when we say a "lower vibrational energy," we are talking about a source that is denser than most, and in a lot of ways sturdier, and is more in tune with the physical world we inhabit, since the planet Earth is the densest of all. Well, at least to people living here. This is one of the reasons why it can be so effective and leave such an impact. Technically, our bodies are lower vibrational too, as what they are made of is denser than our spirit. This also means that naturally consciousness is a higher vibration in general. When we put two and two together, we see that if someone stews in their own bitterness and jealousy aimed at you, they are choosing to immerse themselves in lower vibrational energy, and then direct it at you. This is initiated from them and follows the path of least resistance to you, so it arrives directly, through whatever means is best appropriate. If you read between the lines here, you learn a more esoteric example of this. This is also how someone who doesn't know much about energy manipulation can still send negative energy your way. They simply think of you, project their lower vibrational energy into their thoughts, and like a heat seeking rocket, it will find you. From time to time there are stories that illustrate this. An example that comes from mind is when you think to yourself about someone you know who you find annoying: "I wish they would just die!" Then the next time you hear anything about them, you find that they died shortly after you had that thought. Yes, that is one form of psychic attack, and as you can tell, this is an example of how it can happen without the attacker realizing what they are doing.

Here is another example of an unintended/unaware psychic attack, and this is one of my favorites. Let's say you are one of the few from your family who is not Christian, and you have a zealot of an aunt, and every time she sees you, she says, "I always pray for you when I go to church." That, my friends, is an unintended psychic attack, because it is fueled by worry energy, and worry energy is lower vibration energy because it is rooted in fear. Even though this aunt may not mean you any harm, she is, actually, fearing for you, and that is a form of negativity, because she is fearing the unknown. Because what you do is different, then by Jove, it *must* be from the devil! Ha! One of the ways this may manifest is that every Sunday morning when she goes to church, you feel sick to your stomach. Remember, though, that if you are not particularly close to her, or empathic, you might not feel anything at all. But even if you don't feel anything, that doesn't mean nothing is happening. This is one of the many reasons why it is wise to keep up your cleansings and banishings continually. You never know who is sending what kind of energy your way, so it is better to be proactive when it comes to protecting yourself, than being reactive and having to deal with it on the back end, as they say. You can also deduce from all of this material *how* to give psychic attacks, but that is a conversation for another book at another time.

Now that we've looked at two examples of unintended psychic attacks, let's look at a few ways in which attacks may manifest upon you. The first, and least reliable method of detection, is a gut feeling that you are being attacked. Why is it unreliable, you may ask? Unless you are highly skilled and experienced, you run the risk of projecting your own fears and perspectives onto a situation that has nothing to do with a psychic attack. For example, just because you had a bad day it doesn't mean you were psychically assaulted. Furthermore, if you have a bad day, come home, and upon reflection you think you are being attacked, you probably aren't, because you are projecting that view onto a situation that is most likely not there, creating your own headaches in the process, which means the karma falls on your shoulders ultimately.

Some people simply feel a throbbing in the skull, much like a migraine headache, while others may get nauseous when under assault. If you are an adept clairvoyant, you may get a message in the form of a visual impression of someone attacking you. But here again, this could be self-delusion. If you do get a visual of something like this, be very, very skeptical, and cut the situation with Occam's Razor. If there's no reason for you to be psychically attacked, then you probably aren't. If you are in line with your ascended self and the universe, you may see signs when you are out in public that are telling you that you are being attacked, but here again, this technique is really only worth its salt if you are a developed person.

I realize this chapter is smaller than the others, but that is because a lot of this is covered throughout the book. The intention of this chapter is simply to give a point of reference and background to those that may not be familiar with a psychic attack.

Chapter Three
Semiprecious Stones

One of the most common, effective, popular, and cost-effective tools out there is the use of semiprecious stones to add to your protection repertoire. Also known as gemstones, these can be of great use to you in a very low maintenance way. Stones, as they are commonly called, have been used for thousands of years in various spiritual and cultural contexts all over the globe. Their use in ancient Egypt and the Middle East catapulted them into the Western mass consciousness, and it is through early writings that their use has been continued to this day.

The study of semiprecious stones is known as gemology, and this field is oftentimes linked with geology, due to the fact that they are found in and under the earth. Not every gemologist works with the stones' metaphysical properties though, and sometimes this can be good, because they will price stones based on their non-metaphysical value. Other times though, this can be not so good, especially if a stone merchant discounts metaphysics. What this means is that when you are "rock shopping," it would be wise to know what kind of person you are dealing with, because this will affect not only prices, but also what kind of experience you have overall. I know many people who have stopped at rock shops looking for stones for their metaphysical properties, only to be surprised when they find that they are dealing with someone who doesn't 'believe' in metaphysics and related subjects. This is a detail point really, but it bears keeping in mind to protect yourself from possible negative experiences with the proprietor.

Because gemology is scientific study, there is inevitably a hard science aspect to it, but most metaphysical books do not go into detail about this side of stones. This information is readily found in more scientific oriented books and resources, though, so it is not that hard to acquire. There are some metaphysicians who include this information in their books and let this point be of use to you when it comes to picking quality books on the subject from a metaphysical perspective. In this book I will give the chemical compound of the stones we discuss. Sometimes this information can be useful because it can tell you if there are any toxic components in the stones you want to use. And, along the scientific lines of things, it should also be considered that sometimes a stone's toxicity only comes out when activated. Usually this occurs by getting the stone wet. For example, the stone malachite. By itself it is quite safe to hold, but if you put it in water to make a gemstone elixir, it can be toxic in large quantities. This underscores the point that you should do your research before working with any stones. Most stones are safe, but there are some you will come across that are not, so it is wise to not always to trust your intuition alone with them. Your intuition will tell you whether or not you should work with them, but further information can give you guidance on *how* it would be safe to work with them.

Stones are quite popular because in some ways they are about as low maintenance as you can get. They all have particular vibrations, and this gives them a basic level of consciousness, too. They are sentient, but nowhere near as developed as an animal or a human. They belong to the mineral kingdom, and of course are some of the oldest tools at our disposal. They absorb and enhance surrounding vibrations, or can change extenuating vibrations, depending on the stone. Stones have varying degrees of consciousness based on the vibration they carry, and this is generally reflected in the density of the material that constitutes the stone. The heavier and denser the stone, the more manifested the properties. For example, the traits of various jasper stones are of a more physical plane nature than the traits of an ametrine, which is generally physically lighter and more translucent in appearance. Many stones are kept out of sunlight for concern their color might fade, while others are wise to keep dry. A lot of this varies from stone to stone, so it is wise to do research when you begin working with them, as I said above. Really the only regular maintenance they require is energetical cleansing. Oh, and give them a rest every now and then. Like people, stones need periods of rest to recharge.

The Care and Feeding of Your Gemstones

Technically, how you clean your gemstones is entirely up to you. Most people use white sage to smudge them, but some use copal, dragon's blood or even frankincense and myrrh incenses, passing the stone through the smoke. If you are familiar with smudging techniques, then you already know how this works. For those of you who are not, here is a quick overview. Light whatever it is you want to use as your smudging instrument. When you have a good trail of smoke flowing, pick up the gemstone and pass it through the smoke. While you are doing this, you can say a prayer for cleansing it if you wish. Or you can visualize white light coming down from above to cleanse it. This is a highly subjective process that should be performed in line with your spiritual tradition. Regarding this point, there is no technical right or wrong way, as long as you show reverence for what you are doing, respecting the stone, and not behaving in a flippant manner under the pretense of ritual. After you feel that the stone has been cleansed, extinguish the smoke and either put your stone away, or keep it on you, depending on your intent.

Another method that has been mostly an oral tradition is to set your stones out in a spot in the home where they can absorb the light from a full moon. So yes, this requires a full moon in order to do this. There are a couple of details to make note of though, which should be kept in mind if you're looking at using this technique. The first point is that this does mean you have to take all of your stones outside and put them in direct moonlight. Of course, yes, this is the preferred way to go, but it is not the only way. You could put your stones on a window ledge, for example, as long as the moonlight streaming in can bathe them. The second point is practicality. Bluntly, I don't have the ability to take all of my stones out for charging each month because I have so many, and I know others in the same situation. Or it could be that your stones are too big to move by yourself. No matter the reason, this should be kept in mind when you are thinking about how and when to cleanse them. Be smart with it. Don't feel like you have to conform to any official preset ways, because there are none. Since I can't take my stones out every month, I only recharge the ones I've been working with routinely. Often I will also charge a stone in the full moon for use afterwards. Think through how you want to handle this and do as thou wilt.

Before we progress, I would like to interject a quick note here about the correspondences and traits of gemstones. Their characteristics, correspondences, and attributes have been arrived at by a couple of different ways over the centuries. The first is that their traits have been passed down through the centuries, and logically it stands to reason that the traits attributed to them are simply lists of effects that have been noticed when people worked with them routinely over time. The other method is that people have meditated while with the stone, and the focus of that meditation was to make contact with the stone and learn about what it has to teach us. As you can see, this is a highly subjective method, but is one that is commonly utilized none the less. So for those of you who were wondering how all of these traits came to be, there you go. Each stone also has a hardness factor, which is exactly what it says it is. This is known as the Mohs system of hardness (devised by the German mineralogist Friedrich Mohs in 1812). This represents the density and solidness of each stone, up to a hardness of 10. The lower the number, the softer the stone. Chakra astrological correspondences have all been correlated to them as well.

Moving on from their maintenance, let's talk about stones themselves. They can be communicated with, and while I prefer verbally talking to them, you can use the power of your mind to contact them. Your ability to communicate with them is based upon your natural psychic abilities. As I discussed in my book *Spirit Relations*, we are all psychic, but what varies is *how* we are, and to what degree. Some people will just intuitively feel their stones, while others may go so far as to hear voices coming from the stones they work with. On top of this, some stones are highly enough evolved to be programmable, as is the case of clear quartz.

Clear Quartz

Clear quartz is the highest evolved stone in the mineral kingdom. It is so powerful and evolved that it is used in every computer on the planet. You can also program it for different effects. If you want it to protect you, then you can meditate with it or in some other way energetically charge it to align with your intent, and that's all it takes. When you're done with using it for that purpose, you can cleanse the programming and replace it with something else. Naturally, clear quartz is an energy amplifier, so you can put it with other stones to enhance their attributes. This is what makes it the most versatile stone in your repertoire.

Most other stones are specialized in their functions though, and in some ways since they are more focused, they can be more powerful. Scientifically, clear quartz is: SiO_2, and is silicon dioxide. Its hardness level is 7.

Rutilated Quartz

Rutilated quartz is another good stone to work with because it is an energy amplifier similar to clear quartz. However, it amplifies the stones around it, whereas clear quartz amplifies whatever energy you give it, or that it comes into contact with, thus making rutilated quartz more like an amplifier in general. It is basically the same as clear quartz but has golden rutiles in it. These are made of titanium dioxide and are often called "The Hairs of Venus." There are other similar stones to this as well, and one of them bears examination after we finish this discussion. The rutiles in the stone are known as *inclusions*, and many stones possess these. Not all inclusions are physical artifacts like rutiles though; some are natural formations within the stone that appear to be something special, such as images of angels, faeries, etc. Scientifically, rutilated quartz is SiO_2, silicon dioxide with titanium, which are the inclusions. Its hardness is 7 as well.

Tourmalinated Quartz

This stone is a combination of the concept of rutilated quartz and black tourmaline, which we will discuss a little later. In short, tourmalinated quartz is clear quartz, but the infusions in it are black tourmaline, rather than the rutiles mentioned previously. Black tourmaline is the stone that repels that which is not of the light, and when it is found in clear quartz like this, its effect is amplified. Thus, it is basically a more powerful version of black tourmaline. Therefore, scientifically, it is SiO_2, and is silicon dioxide, with tourmaline inclusions, and its hardness is 7.

Smoky Quartz

Next in the quartz family of protection stones to discuss is smoky quartz. We slightly shift our focus here, as this stone is highly alchemical in nature. Using smoky quartz assists you to change negative energy into positive energy. You can see that this deviates from the concept of a protector stone and bridges the gap into the transmutation of energy. Often, it is easier to change the energy around you rather than pit your Will against it in the name of safety. After all, the energy being sent to you is free energy, and you have control over what you do with it. The reason this type of quartz is smoky is because it has been radiated from the stones around it over the course of extended periods of time. This radiation is not harmful to us, though. It is worth noting that smoky quartz has gotten scarcer over the years, and because of that, many specimens you will find have been artificially radiated to produce the deep smoky color. It can lift depression and assist with bringing positive energy to a situation. It is the same as above, SiO_2, with a hardness of 7.

Blood Quartz

The lesser known blood quartz can be of great use as well when it comes to protection magick. No, it does not have blood in it, but what it does contain is just as valuable when it comes to protection magick. In it is found hematite, a stone long and widely known to absorb negativity. This works much the same as tourmalinated quartz, in that the surrounding quartz amplifies the natural properties of hematite. This makes it a great stone for absorbing negative energy that may come your way on any given day. Since it is in the immediate quartz family, it is SiO_2, with a hardness of 7, and has hematite inclusions.

Now we'll step away from the quartz family and broaden our perspective to look at other stones that have protective properties. There are some that will be on this list that are not specifically protective stones per se, but they have properties that can be worked with in the name of cleanliness and protection. The way the stones are listed will be in order of importance from my perspective. And away, we go!

Black Tourmaline

Tourmaline is really an entire family of stones, ranging in a variety of colors, even to the degree that there is one that is an amalgamation (watermelon tourmaline) of several. This is a classic stone for protection, as it repels that which is not of the light. This is very important to keep in mind because when you decide to work with it, certain people or situations in your life will oftentimes leave or diminish, and these may be ones you didn't expect! Yet, you may find that their diminishment improves your life, and this is the way black tourmaline works. It repels negative vibrations, but it does not discriminate, and it takes humility on our part to trust that the stone is doing its work. It has a hardness factor ranging from 7-7.5, and its chemical composition is $XY_3Z_6 (T_6O_{18})(BO_3)_3V_3W$. It has a definitive appearance as well, as long, deep, parallel lines are found in almost all, if not all, specimens.

Hematite

Hematite is a metallic grey colored stone that feels lighter than you would think when you look at it. It is a very light stone overall and is quite fragile. As a matter of fact, its softness reveals one of its characteristics. It is said that you will always know when a hematite has absorbed all of the negative energy it can take, because it will break. Sometimes in jewelry settings the stone won't break, but the piece will simply disappear. This also means you should be careful in general when handling it, because if you drop it you may accidentally break it, which would cause negativity! It has a chemical composition of Fe_2O_3 and has a hardness factor of somewhere between 5 and 6.5.

Labradorite

Labradorite is a chatoyant, (meaning that reflections from inclusions in the stone cause bands of bright luster to appear within it), translucent green and blue stone that refracts light, which often produces the appearance of a rainbow in the stone. This is a very valuable stone because it seals the aura against energy leaks and leeches, making it a fantastic anti-vampire stone. When you look at it, it resembles a quartz rather than a black tourmaline or a hematite. Its hardness factor is surprisingly about the same as hematite, which is interesting to me, because I have heard of more pieces of hematite breaking than I have labradorite. Its chemical formula is $NaAlASi_3O_8$, but there are variances that are known.

Unakite

A lesser known but very powerful stone is unakite. Aesthetically, it may not have the appeal of some of the other stones discussed here, but energetically it is quite profound. Unakite keeps your energy clear when in close proximity to negative people. You can see why this is so appealing! If you are getting ready to go into a situation where you will be surrounded by negative people, then this is the stone for you. This is one of my favorite stones for that reason. Because of these properties, thus making its use so specialized, you really only have to work with it when the situation merits it, so it can get plenty of rest to stay fresh. But then again, if you find you are using it more often than not, you may want to do some inner reflection and look in the mirror. It has a hardness factor of 5.5, and its structure is $\{Ca_2\}\{Al_2Fe^{3+}\}(Si_2O_7)(SiO_4)O(OH)$.

Turquoise

This is one of the classic protection stones going back hundreds of years. It is opaque, and ranges in color from aquamarine to sea foam green, to a darker shade of light blue. It has been used in cultures all over the world in various ways, ranging from jewelry to makeup pigmentation, but is usually associated with Native American cultures. It is excellent for psychic protection as well as maintaining a good state of well-being. It is also a healing stone, specifically when it comes to emotional and spiritual healing. On a physical level, turquoise detoxifies the body and addresses other maladies, but its focus on psychic protection is why it's mentioned here. It has a hardness factor of between 5-6, and its structure is 4H2O. Notice the connection to the structure of water (H2O). This shows a strong connection not only to water, but also then, by default, to our bodies. Since it is one of the most popular stones in use today, much has been written about it, so it is easy to find more material for those who are interested.

Ruby

Another stone that can be found throughout time and across cultures is ruby. Ranging from pink to blood red, it is a variety of corundum, meaning it shares a connection with sapphire. It is known as one of the stones of nobility. When it comes to protective properties, it gives a general protection, but specifically protects the wearer from plagues and pestilence. More broadly, it also offers protection for the physical form in general. In addition, it protects against bad dreams and offers defense when it comes to affairs of the heart. Its hardness factor is a 9, and its structure is AI2O3Cr.

Lapis Lazuli

My personal favorite stone, lapis lazuli (Lapis for short) is similar to ruby and turquoise in that it is commonly found in ancient cultures from many different places and is known to be one of the more powerful stones that have been used throughout history. It ranges in color from light blue to a deep, night sky blue. Usually it has golden flecks in it, giving it a starry appearance. It is opaque, and sometimes contains veins of milky white. The white comes from calcite, and the gold flecksare pyrite inclusions. Protectively, it is said to give the wearer psychic protection and facilitates astral travel. It also offers protection from the evil eye and negativity in general. It works extensively with the development of higher consciousness and can thus shield the wearer against negative thoughts and vibrations. It has a hardness factor of 5-6, and its structure is (NaCa)8 (AISiO4)6, (S, SO4CI)1. Complex, yeah, I know, but that is because lapis is a rock, not a crystalline structure as other stones we've been discussing.

Amethyst

Another popular stone, amethyst is generally known for its common moniker of being the stone of sobriety, or perhaps its ability to stimulate the third eye and clairvoyance. However, what is not as well-known are its protective properties. These aren't traditional, though, in that it doesn't shield you from psychic attacks, etc. Rather it is protective because it is an energy cleanser. And since it corresponds to the Ajna chakra, it can be seen as protective

Psychic Protection

in the way that it stimulates the clairvoyance faculty, putting you in a position of empowerment. The energy cleansing properties it has allow the user to cleanse themselves of any toxic energy they may have encountered during the day, so in this way, amethyst is more of a detoxifier. Be careful with it though, as it will fade if exposed to too much sunlight. It is generally a deep purple color, especially the strains coming from South America, and is chatoyant. Its hardness factor is generally a 7 but will be lower if it is not top quality. Its structure is $SiO2$, and it is a member of the quartz family.

Prehnite

Green prehnite is an interesting selection for protective stones, because it's not so much protective in nature as preventative. But as we all know, being proactive is better than being reactive. Working with green prehnite helps you empower your precognitive skills so that you can anticipate things that are coming your way. This addresses not only precognition, but also enhancing your intuitive skills. It has a hardness factor of around 6, and its structure is $Ca2A(AlSi3O10)$.

Carnelian

Carnelian is another stone that you might think does not belong on this list, but it does have protective qualities that are worth mentioning here. A form of chalcedony, carnelian is generally considered a stone of sensuality, and with its chatoyant orange reddish appearance, it is easy to see why. In addition to these properties, though, it also grants the bearer courage and physical power. This is another stone that has been use in various cultures dating back to antiquity, and because of that, includes many more properties beyond the scope of this work, but are worth noting nonetheless. When it comes to psychic protection though, the granting of courage and prowess are the two of the most important qualities you can possess. It has a hardness factor of 7, and its chemical makeup is $SiO2$.

Gold Tiger's Eye

Commonly known as simply "tiger's eye," this deep brown stone with gold striations is generally considered a masculine stone, but mostly due to its beauty and composition more than anything else. It is quite a popular and powerful stone and has a red variation. Red tiger's eye is not as common though, and its traits carry it out of the purview of this text. Gold tiger's eye is a stone that assists with providing the bearer with strength, willpower, stamina, fortitude, and courage. Thus, you can see how it can be a fantastic stone ally. It has a hardness of 7, and its structure is $SiO2$. At this point, it is wise to note the common reoccurring $SiO2$ mentioned in this chapter. This is because so many stones are related, geologically speaking. What separates them on a scientific level are details outside the parameters of this book, but I do feel it is important to mention this here for the sake of clarity.

Tiger Iron

Related to tiger's eye, tiger iron is similar in the traits it can provide. The stone itself is a combination of gold tiger's eye, hematite, iron, and red jasper, which we will discuss shortly. It has properties similar to gold tiger's eye, and in addition to those, it also grants the bearer refuge when going through periods of intense change. The hematite also aids in absorbing negativity, and because of the other properties of the stone, can assist in transmuting the negative into positive. It has a hardness factor of somewhere between 6.5-7, and its structure is $SiO2$ and $Fe2O3$.

Amazonite

Amazonite is a very interesting and powerful stone and its importance should not be understated. It is known as the stone of courage and of truth. It is also the stone of overcoming loneliness, as well as dissipating negativity and aggravation. In addition to these traits, it also filters out geostress, absorbing electromagnetic pollution, microwaves, and the energy from cellphones. Geostress in this context refers to how natural energies get distorted when they come into contact with humans, and how these changes adversely affect the human condition. It also helps ward against people that try and take advantage of you. Its sea-green color makes it a fit for most fashion trends, whether jewelry or clothing, and its opaque nature makes it one that is good for grounding, in addition to everything else mentioned. It has a hardness factor of somewhere between 5.5-6, and has a composition of $KALSi3O8$.

Sugilite

Another opaque stone, sugilite is a beautiful dark blue or lightly purple stone with striations of white in it. While most of its qualities have to do with concepts other than protection, there is one significant trait that aligns it with this text, in that it helps you to accept the here and now, so it is very pragmatic and practical in that regard. It has a hardness factor of 6-6.57, and its structure is $KNa2(Fe, Mn, AI)2Li3Si12O30$.

Jet

Technically, jet is not a semiprecious stone, but rather it is petrified wood. However, for all practical purposes, it is used interchangeably as such. It is also related to the coal family, and the bulk of jet comes from Russia. It is good for grounding, purification, and protection, as is indicated by its black color. It is a soft stone though, so you would be wise to keep this in mind while working with it. It is also good at cleansing the aura. Another subtle feature is that it can help those who are working through grief. It has a hardness factor of somewhere between 2.5-4, and its structure is C1H1O-2H2O.

Zebra Stone/Zebra Marble

Alternatively known as aebra stone or zebra marble, it is technically related to the jasper family, which we will discuss in a moment. It is named as such because of its black and white stripes and is generally opaque. It is usually white with black stripes, but there are also variations that occur. It is good for increasing your energy and vitality, as well as healing. It is also appropriate for grounding and manifesting your Will. It promotes creativity, stability, and security. It is a softer stone, having a hardness factor between 3-3.5, and its structure is $SiO2$.

The Jasper Family

Really, jasper is a family of stones rather than just one stone, so it is almost impossible to cover it all here. And even if I tried, some of the information would be beyond the scope of psychic protection. Rather than going through all of the stones in the family, I will only focus on a few here that are specifically pertinent to psychic protection. This concept is also true of the agate stones. They are a family just like the jaspers, but only a few are specifically appropriate for psychic protection. We will discuss the agates in a moment, but for now, let's discuss a few jaspers that are good for psychic protection: fancy jasper and starry jasper.

Fancy jasper is good for strength, courage,

determination, and harmony. It is also appropriate for bringing harmony and alignment between an individual and their environment. It is a varied stone, ranging in colors and patterns from light blue/borderline white all the way to shades of black or dark red. It is also a good stone for tranquility. Its opaqueness is overshadowed by the "fanciness" of its appearance. It has a hardness factor of 7, and its structure is $SiO2$.

Related to fancy jasper is starry jasper, which shares a lot of the same properties as other stones in the Jasper family, including F=fancy jasper, but it differs in that it is good for protection, especially when traveling. It can also assist with being grounded and healing. It is known as "starry" because it often contains pyrite inclusions, which appear as gold in the stone itself. To give you a perspective on pyrite, it is also known as "fool's gold" due to its golden appearance. This gold shines through in starry jasper, making it quite attractive. It has a hardness factor ranging between 6.5-7, and its structure is $SiO2$.

The Agate Family

Agate is like jasper in that there are many, many variations of it, and while they often vary regarding their properties, they have many in common. This is also true of their chemical makeup. For our purposes, there is one main agate to discuss, and that is turritella agate. One of the things to keep in mind is that the agate family is full of color and bright, vivid striations. One of the unique characteristics of turritella agate is that it contains fossils, which enhance its natural brown color. It ranges from deep brown to lighter shades of brown, yet they all contain fossils of some sort. Turritella agate is also translucent in nature, which is a trait that is commonly found in the agate family. It has a hardness factor of 6.5-7, and its structure is $SiO2$, relating it to a lot of stones that have been discussed up to this point.

Bill Duvendack

The Aventurine Family

Another family of stones that is broad and varied is the aventurine family. Most people that are reading this are probably familiar with green aventurine due to the fact that it is known as a stone of abundance and good health, but fewer might be familiar with one of its relatives: red aventurine. Yes, there are many more aventurine stones than just these two, but these are the type of interest in respect of psychic protection. Red aventurine is, as you may have suspected, red in color, and usually it is an opaque red. It ranges from light red to deep red. This is an interesting stone when it comes to psychic protection because its qualities and traits are concerned with taking action, vitality, commitment, discernment, and executing good judgment. It is red due to the inclusion of hematite, which also reveals it is good for absorbing negativity. It has a hardness factor of 6.5, and its structure is $SiO2$.

The Obsidian Family

The final family to address here is that of obsidian. Really, the fact it is considered a stone is a little bit misleading, as it is technically volcanic glass. It comes in a variety of colors, but black obsidian is the variety that most applies to this subject. As I've made clear in this chapter, black stones are generally seen as protective stones, and black obsidian is no exception. It is good for clearing muddled energy, protection, grounding, clearing, and overall cleansing. It is light to the touch and can be almost translucent. It can also help you to get to the bottom of any negative patterns you may have, and as we know, when we uncover these things, we are in a position of empowerment to raise our vibration, which is the best protection of all. It has a hardness factor of 5.5, and its structure is $SiO2$.

I realize this list could be added to by people who are more familiar with gem stones than I am, but it is my intention for this to be a quick reference point for those who are just starting to work with stones as a method of protection. When in doubt, remember that black stones are protective in general, and they can also assist with staying grounded. Feel free to do your own research when it comes to stones. One of the most beneficial characteristics of stones is that they can be very specialized, so while a lot of these are general protective stones, you can also see that some have highly specific properties. This is worth keeping in mind because you may find a rare stone that addresses a certain kind of protection that fits your specific situation, and it may be more powerful than a general protection stone mentioned here. If this occurs, adjust your application and work accordingly.

Chapter Four
A Protection Apothecary

Another popular and common physical tool to use for psychic protection are herbs, and derivatives of them, such as oils. Many books have been written on those topics over the years, and some from the perspective of science, while others from the perspective of metaphysics, and still others, a blending of the two. Because of that, I am going to tackle this subject similarly to my discussion of stones. I will let you know up front this is not a "be all end all" book on herbs, but rather what you find in here will be sufficient for the purposes of psychic protection.

Unlike most stones though, there is a huge point to note, which is before you use any herbs, oils, or other derivatives, DO YOUR RESEARCH! Many herbs, and therefore their extractions and variants, can cause serious health issues, either immediately or through extended use. Some may work fine for some people, while for other people they cause severe health issues, so always, always, always, research an herb before you use it, regardless of what people might tell you about it. Also of note is that some herbs are okay in one form, but in another they are potentially hazardous. When in doubt, consult a certified professional in the field, and even then, double check their credentials. In this day and age, having certification or a degree doesn't amount to much, due to the influence of the Internet and its culture. As a matter of fact, the cynic in me says that really, education and certification don't amount to much in most cases, as anyone can be certified in anything, but I would also say that is not necessarily

Psychic Protection

completely true here. We are talking about your physical health after all, and that is not a subject to be taken lightly. This can make working with herbs more challenging than working with stones because of the research time involved. However, herbs are a lot more flexible and adaptable, so they can be used in a variety of ways, more so than semiprecious stones. This also means that if someone can't work with a particular herb or derivative, then it is on them to find an alternative. Too many times people use their inability to work with an herb as an excuse to be disempowered, and that is one of unfortunately common tragedies today. It is actually the opposite of psychic protection.

Keep in mind that all herbs do not grow in all places, which may impact your ability to acquire them in your local area. If this is the case, you can research alternatives. Like so many things in magick it is always better if you can grow your own, but if you can't, that is quite alright, too. It is wise to buy herbs if you can't grow them, rather than go without at all. Basic science should be considered in this discussion too, as some herbs can't grow in particular environments. Further, some herbs are endangered, so you should consider the ethics involved in acquiring herbs that may be endangered. It is fairly easy to find alternatives to some of the herbs discussed here, because the common correspondence is that they should be predicated around psychic protection. Unlike stones, usually the characteristics of herbs are general rather than specific. For example, when discussing protective stones, a stone may help you transmute negativity, which is a form of protection, but you would be hard pressed to find an herb that specifically did that. In some ways, this is a good thing, as it means it is easier to find herbs that work with you and for you. The drawback, of course, is that this makes herbs more generic, but more applicable. For example, chamomile. It is good for relaxation and helping you sleep.

For contrast, the stone rose quartz is also good for promoting sleep, but specifically for gently falling asleep rather than just "knocking you out," as chamomile often time does.

Finally, in the following herb list, you will see that the Latin name is mentioned. I have included this because not everyone who reads this will be English speakers, and thus by including the Latin names, it makes it easier to find the proper translation in your native tongue. I have learned this over the years through experience. In other words, it creates a baseline for all of us to use. You will also notice that some things on this list are not herbs in the strictest definition of the word, but I put them here because generally they're lumped together in resources having to do with psychic protection. Things like myrrh, which is the gum from a tree, are included, too. All of these are listed in alphabetical order for your convenience. After we get through this list, we will discuss different applications of this information, so you will see they are just as, if not more so, flexible as stones, which stands to reason. Keep in mind that this is not a completely comprehensive list, and you may come across herbs that are not on here that you can use for protective purposes. Feel free to add them to your personal journal in addition to what you find here. It is almost impossible to make a fully comprehensive list, because some herbs are only found in one spot on the globe, and therefore one would have to visit every square inch of the planet AND learn all of the herbs found there, AND discover their protective properties, in order to establish a be all and end all list, and that would take a lifetime or two to complete. That is the reason why I will not even attempt it here. It would be a fool's errand to attempt that in this text. Anyway, enough of the background and context. Let's begin!

Common Name	Latin Name	Planet
Aloe Vera	*Aloe perfoliata*	The Moon
Angelica Root	*Angelica archangelica*	The Sun
Anise Seed or Star	*Pimpinella anisum*	Jupiter
Balm of Gilead	*Cammiphora opobalsamum*	Venus
Bamboo	*Bambusoideae*	
Basil	*Ocimum basilicum*	Mars
Bay/Bay Laurel	*Laurus nobilis*	Sun
Blackberry	*Rubus*	Venus
Bloodroot	*Sanguinaria*	Mars
Blueberry	*Cyanococcus*	
Bodhi Seed	*Ficus religiosa*	Jupiter
Burdock Root	*Arctium*	Venus
Cactus	*Cactaceae*	
Carnation	*Dianthus caryophyllus*	The Sun
Cedar	*Cedrus*	The Sun
Chrysanthemum	*Chrysanthemum*	The Sun
Clove	*Syzygium aromaticum*	Jupiter
Cumin	*Cuminum cyminum*	Mars
Dragon's Blood Resin	*Dracaena* (There are many variations of it beyond this)	Mars
Fern	*Polypodiopsida*	Mercury
Frankincense Tears	*Boswellia*	The Sun
Garland	*Chrysanthemum coronarium*	
Garlic	*Allium sativum*	Mars
Honeysuckle	*Lonicera*	Jupiter
Hyssop	*Hyssopus officinalis*	Jupiter
Ivy	*Hedera*	Saturn
Juniper	*Juniperus*	The Sun
Lilac	*Syringa*	Venus
Lily	*Lilium*	The Moon
Lucky Hand Root	*Orchis* (There are many variations beyond this)	Venus
Mandrake Root	*Mandragora officinarum*	Mercury
Mint	*Mentha*	Mercury
Mugwort	*Artemisia vulgaris*	Venus
Mullein	*Verbascum*	Saturn
Nettle	*Urtica dioica*	Mars
Oak	*Quercus*	The Sun
Pennyroyal	*Mentha pulegium*	Mars
Peony	*Paeonia*	The Sun

Bill Duvendack

Pine	*Pinus*	Mars
Raspberry	*Rubus idaeus*	Venus
Sage	*Salvia officinalis* (And there are more types)	Jupiter
Sea Salt	*Sodium chloride*	
Tulips	*Tulipa*	Venus

When they are known, I have included the planets that particular herbs correspond to, but you will notice there are some that don't have planetary correspondences. There are various reasons for this, and in the future perhaps there will be correspondences, but as of right now I couldn't find any. This doesn't mean they aren't out there though, but considering we're focused on the herbs for protection, knowing the planetary correspondences is secondary. Let's take a closer look at the above list, because not all herbs are created equal.

The first thing you may notice is that not everything on that list is technically an herb. Roots, a seed, and resins are also listed. Even though they are different, I include them here because in a broad sense, all of them derive from and reside in the natural kingdom. In the above list there are basically four categories, if you want to call them that. There are standard herbs, roots, resins, and salt. All of them should be researched before use, but the different types can give rise to different applications. There are also different ways to work with them, too. Regular herbs don't really require much explanation beyond what we have already discussed, so let's look at the other groups.

Let's start with the roots that are listed above. For all practical purposes, they are functionally the same as the regular herbs. The list above contains three roots: angelica root, burdock root, and lucky hand root. The main difference only applies if you are going to make *tinctures*, which we will discuss shortly. What this means is that if you are going to make an herbal pouch, they can be put in there with the regular herbs and can have the same results.

Psychic Protection

The same is true with the resins mentioned above, regarding their use in a protective pouch. In the above list, there are three resins listed: balm of Gilead, frankincense, and dragon's blood. Resins are secreted by various plants, usually trees, and are often used as incenses, either burned on charcoal tablets or in joss stick form. We will talk about incense a little later, too. The other odd ball on the list is an obvious one, which is sea salt. There's not a lot to discuss here about that, other than to say it has been used for a long time for cleansing and protection. I simply point it out here to clarify the above table. Now that we have established a working list, let us move on to discuss the various applications.

Pouches and Poppets

Much has been written about both of these topics over the years, and I see no reason to retread trodden ground. We will take a few minutes to discuss both of them though, as they are appropriate to the overall book. Carrying herbs in pouches is something that goes back thousands of years across the globe in many different cultures, and the premise is simple: carry herbs on your person for various ends. In some cases they were carried to be taken internally at a later time. In others, they were carried for the effects they could produce just by being in the auric field of the carrier. Sometimes this was a form of sympathetic magick, where the carrier believed that the herbs were symbolic, and thus being surrounded by them could produce various effects. Sometimes though, it was not sympathetic magick at all, but rather based on the knowledge of the carrier. For example, the carrier knew what the herbs were good for, and had them on their person for that reason. To clarify, one might know that when they carried a flower like lilacs on them, that while they smelled better, they were also treated differently by the people they contacted. Tradition says it is always best to make your own pouch, and while I agree with that, if that is not your skill set, it is perfectly acceptable to buy a premade pouch. The secret to working with herbs that are carried in a pouch is to keep them in your auric field. Usually this means in a pocket, but if you do not have pockets, you might have to get creative. I know many women who carry a pouch in their bra, as an example. Some herbs are more specific though. When I was much younger, I learned you should carry mullein leaf in your shoe for safe travel. While yes, it was messy, I also saw it always worked! In American Hoodoo and African-Caribbean practices this is discussed extensively, and those would be your starting points.

Poppets on the other hand, are lesser known, but quite powerful. Usually you will find information about them from the same sources you consult for pouches, so it should be no issue to acquire more detailed, advanced information about them if you desire. The gist of a poppet is that it is roughly the shape of a person. You can make them as detailed as you want, though, which means you could make a poppet in the form of a male or a female. The next step is to fill it with appropriate ingredients. There are many different materials you can employ for this, ranging from bone powder to what is more appropriate to our discussion: herbs. Sometimes people will consecrate a poppet to a particular person, in the case of the pedestrian view of "Voodoo Dolls," and magically, the idea is often to control or guide another person. The stereotypical image that comes to mind is the doll that gets stuck with pins in order to cause another person pain. When it comes to psychic protection, though, the application of the poppet is quite different. One of the ways you can use a poppet for protective purposes is to fill it with an appropriate herb, or herbs, and then put it in your sacred space (or at least a safe place) in your home. Consecrate it to give you protection, and leave it be for however long you choose. This works

Psychic Protection

on the belief that it is a representative of your spirit. Thus, while you are out and about living life, this poppet is protecting you from a distance. Remember that energy knows no distance. Using a poppet this way dates back to predynastic Egypt, so it is time-tested and a global technique. Remember the basic rules of creation when you use this technique, though. You can also consecrate the poppet to someone other than yourself, and thus the individual would receive the protective energy from the herbs contained within it.

Incense

The burning of incense, i.e. herbs and/or resins, on some sort of fire is another application that goes back thousands of years, cross-culturally and globally. Many herbs have been used as incenses over the years, and these range from natural blends, such as what you would find in potpourri, to blending them with some sort of carrier, placed on a stick, and burned that way. A carrier is something that is used to bind various substances together. Some of the ones listed above, though, are resins, and they require a little bit of discussion.

Generally speaking, resins are secretions such as sap that come from various trees. An exception to this is amber, but that is a conversation for another time. Resins are very easy to use as incenses due to their naturally sticky nature, and while they are not technically herbs, often you will find them in the same places as herbs. Most resins are safe to use as is, but at least one in particular, dragon's blood, can be toxic to the touch over an extended period of exposure, which is why it is always important to do your research before using anything in this chapter.

Incenses are so common, whether you believe in their metaphysical properties or not. It has been proven time and again that the olfactory senses have a profound impact on the human psyche, and many people use incense just to aid relaxation, if nothing else. The three common ways incenses are used are either in stick form, burned over charcoal tabs, or burned in cone form. You can see that, whatever form you choose to use, you will most likely need accessories as well. Stick incense needs a container that can hold it up as well as catch the ashes that fall. Cone incense needs to be burned in a flameproof container that can also catch the ashes. Incense burned over charcoal is the highest maintenance, but is the most pungent, and often the most cost effective. You will need the incense, charcoal to burn it on, a flameproof container to burn it in and something to light it with. It is down to personal preference which type of incense you burn, if you should choose to use it. Simply know that it is purely down to personal preference, regardless of what else you might read about it.

Fragrances

Another subject that needs very little to no introduction is the use and application of scented oils. Generally known as *aromatherapy*, oils have been used for thousands of years for various purposes. Commonly, they are used to enhance charisma and attraction, but you can also use them for protective purposes. Most oils are derived from herbs and resins, and from a metaphysical perspective are considered a higher vibration than incenses. They penetrate the finer planes easier and can reach greater heights. There is also the fact that they are generally less pungent than incenses. For those of you who may not be able to tolerate smoke for various reasons, you may find oils are better suited for protective purposes. No matter the case, simply know that oils are a great alternative. Since they are generally more socially acceptable, they can be used in environments that might favor light scents rather than the earthiness of incenses. Another point to remember is that smoke, no

Psychic Protection

matter what kind, is thicker and therefore lingers longer and sticks to clothes and items longer than oils. The scent of oils tends to wear off before that of incense smoke, so you may find you adjust which tool you use in proportion to the event or environment you are in. I have been in several corporate meeting where oils are more appropriate than being covered in incense smoke, as an example. The same health warnings apply here, though, as oils can be as dangerous as some herbs.

Here is an example from many years ago. While working in a metaphysical shop, a regular customer came in wearing a head band. It wasn't his normal style of dress, and when we struck up a conversation with him, we ended up with a lesson. It turns out he had performed a ritual for prosperity since the last time we'd seen him. He did his research and found out that cinnamon oil was good for prosperity, so he drew a pentacle on his forehead as part of the ritual. Well, when applied to the skin, essential cinnamon oil burns, so he ended up with a burnt-in-the-skin pentacle on his forehead! Not only did he suffer the burning sensation from the application, there was also the minor skin irritation that stayed for long after the ritual. All of this because he didn't do thorough research. Even though this was skin irritation, you can imagine how things would have played out differently if there was an allergic reaction that could have caused anaphylactic shock!

Because of this, and for various other reasons, such as environmental consciousness, many people will use artificial fragrances instead of pure essential extracts. Like pouches and poppets, energetically it is always better if you can use the real thing, but if you can't, it will work just as well if you use the artificially made ones. In this day and age, it is actually more responsible to use artificial incenses and oils due to the many endangered species that produce the things we love. For example, frankincense and sandalwood are endangered due to being over harvested because of its popularity, so whenever you get the chance to go with artificial versions of them, it is ethical to do so. While natural is preferred, energetically it makes no difference for all practical purposes.

A newer application of fragrances that can be used almost anywhere are *misters*. Misters are made when you mix an oil with water and some sort of other liquid that helps with cohesion and potency. Thus, you spray yourself or an area with it, and it has the same effect as an oil, but it is much lighter, subtler, and therefore can be used in more places than either oils or incenses. Like the other applications that have been discussed here, it is wise to do your research before simply jumping in to use them. I simply mention them here for the sake of completeness.

Finally, another way that essential oils can be used are through oil *diffusers*. The simplest way to explain this is that a diffuser is some sort of device that contains water. You put a few drops of the desired oil in the water. The next part of a diffuser requires a heat source, because the way it works is that the heat source heats the water, which in turn releases the scent of the oil into the air. I realize I am being vague here with a lot of the details, but that is because there are many ways they are made and used. Some diffusers plug into electrical outlets, which provides the heat source, while other diffusers use a small candle such as a tea light under the water container, which in turn heats the water and activates the oil. Still others can plug into the cigarette lighter of a vehicle and work the same way. Some diffusers will use a cloth or something solid rather than water, but the effect is the same. I know parents who have used the ones that plug into electrical outlets with soothing oils, which can help put their children to sleep or those who suffer from anxiety.

The final way fragrances can be used is through a distillation process known as *tinctures*. These are no strangers to those who are familiar with alchemy, but in

Psychic Protection

recent years have gained widespread popularity due to the spread of witchcraft and Hoodoo. Specifically, a tincture is an extract from a plant that is produced from soaking the plant or plant part in ethanol or a comparable alcohol. This produces a distillation of the essence of the plant. It is more potent than fragrances, as we have discussed before, but generally they are purer. Some people shy away from tinctures though, because they do involve alcohol in some form. Those who have had alcohol problems in the past, for example, prefer to use one of the other methods instead of this one, and as you have probably deduced by now, it really doesn't matter what form of fragrance provider you use, as long as it works for you.

Sometimes, a criticism of working with oils is that they are psychosomatic in nature, meaning that if you know the herb or fragrance is good for protection, then when you are using it, it works because you believe it will. On one hand there is a lot of truth to this, because the mind is more powerful than most people realize or give credit to, but on the other hand, I have seen herbs work to the effects they claim to have, even for people who did not know the effect ahead of time. Let's turn our attention to this end of the spectrum, namely that the herbs actually do have the properties they are purported to have. This is the final application of herbs in this chapter, and another subject that has been written about extensively. This is commonly known as *kitchen witchery*.

Kitchen Witchery

Kitchen witchery is one of my favorite applications of herbs for various reasons. First, anyone can do it. Secondly, it is subtle. Third, while we are discussing it from the perspective of protection, you can use this technique like many of the others listed here, in non-protective ways. So, what exactly *is* kitchen witchery? Yes, it involves a kitchen, which means it also involves cooking and other things you would do in a kitchen. Kitchen witchery is when you cook or in some other way apply the herbs to food and internal consumption to produce desired effects. I know several people who do kitchen witchery that have no other or deeper interest in the occult. They simply know herbs, what they can do, and use that to their advantage. This technique isn't relegated just to food, though, as they can also be used in drinks. For example, often when I am giving a public presentation or teaching a class, I will drink cinnamon coffee. The reason for this is that cinnamon is an herb that promotes prosperity, so I am taking in the idea of prosperity to assist with the success of whatever I am doing. Some people I know will cook their significant other a meal that has calming herbs after a challenging day at work to soothe the vibes in the household. These two examples are but the tip of the iceberg for what you can do with them, and remember that since this is a book on protection, you could use the above list to experiment with, in order to find what works best for you.

Ethics

We haven't discussed what I hinted at yet, though, which is how this works without the idea of psychosomatic effects. I saved this discussion until now because it also requires an examination of ethics. I know several people who have done kitchen witchery without other people knowing it. This isn't common, but it does happen, and quite frequently at that. So, if you are going into a situation that may require protection, you can fix yourself food that includes protective herbs to prepare for what you may encounter. Or conversely, if you know your loved ones are going into those situations, you can make the food for them so that they are extra safe. This is our segue into ethics though, so let's shift gears.

Psychic Protection

To many people, if you do energetic work on or for someone without their knowledge or consent, it is seen as immoral, or at least unethical. It does not require much explanation to see why this is, for the principles are the same as two people having nonconsensual sex. And in a lot of ways, what we are discussing here is so much more intimate because it is spiritual in nature. There are many ways to process this, so let's look at a few of them. First, context must be created in order to fully process this. Let's use the example of a romantic couple. Let's say that one of them practices this skill, while the other one doesn't, but the other is okay with this. If this is the case, then the kitchen witch should have no problem telling their partner what kitchen witchery they are executing. However, if the other does not know their partner does this, and it is done without their permission, then it is easy to see it is practiced non-consensually. While I am a firm believer of Aleister Crowley's wisdom that "ordinary morality is for ordinary people," I also realize not everyone shares that view, so the ethics of using kitchen witchery should be considered before being put into practice. This is especially worth keeping in mind for those of you who read this and are not necessarily interested in other realms of occultism. Rather, you simply know you need energetic protection in your life for one reason or another. This does mean though, that this is another takeaway from this chapter in addition to doing your research on the safety of herbs and oils. Morality and ethics should be considered when you are working with protective techniques, and we will return to this in depth in later chapters. For now, though, simply be aware that with herbs, oils, and the like, ethics should be considered due to the number of applications and ease and convenience of use.

This quick sidebar into ethics is necessary, because I have seen people use the kitchen witchery application of herbs to great effect on those who did not know they were being worked for, and to the desired effect of the herb. This pretty much ruins the idea of the effects of all herbs being one hundred percent psychosomatic, and least logically and to the intelligent. After all, you can't say all herbs and their effects are psychosomatic if they work on a person who doesn't know what effects they will have, or even that they are under the influence at all.

This chapter is brief and an overview, and that is completely intentional. Many authors have written extensively on these subjects, so there are plenty of in depth resources to consult. In this new aeon, a lot of that material has been digitized as well, making it more accessible to those who have a desire to explore and become educated. The intent of this chapter is to be a quick reference guide if you are in a jam and this is the only resource you have. There are usually many different methods to accomplish several of these applications, so you may find conflicting information. For example, you may find multiple ways to make tinctures, and all of them are as equally valid as another. If this becomes the case, trial and error is your friend. After all, all magick, if done correctly, involves trial and error, pioneering and being visionary. There are most likely other ways to work with herbs than those mentioned here, so you may find techniques and applications that come from your own culture and background, and even places on the planet that you visit. If you connect with them, then by all means test them out! Remember to give credit where credit is due, though, so as to avoid passing such techniques off as your own. It is far more impressive to say you learned an obscure technique that works very strongly than it is to try and pass it off as your own. In addition to it being impressive, to be honest is also karmically cleaner and more responsible.

Explore! Experiment! But do your homework! Not all

herbs are created equal, and personal health should be considered first and foremost. If you are unsure about an herb, or your health, then address both. Sometimes an herb might appear safe when you research it, but it turns out you have a reaction to it you didn't know about until you tried it. And, some things change over time. When I first started working in a metaphysical shop, I had no issues with any herbs. However, over time and due to prolonged exposure, I developed a slight allergy to mugwort and wormwood, and even frankincense. So now I have to be careful when I use those three in particular, and I am more cautious before working with herbs in general. Our bodies and their biology change over time, so periodically in our lives we may find we have to put some herbs down in order to work with others that do not harm us. However, *que sera sera*: such is life.

Section Two
Emotional Plane Tools

Chapter Five
Emotional Health and Protection

Like in the previous chapter, I will tread fairly lightly here, because there are trained, certified emotional and psychological health care professionals who should be consulted when it comes to dealing with emotions, and I will always defer to their expertise. They should always be consulted if you are dealing with emotional issues such as the ones we are about to discuss. What we are going to discuss here are broad concepts to keep in mind in the name of protecting yourself emotionally. The reason for this is that not all psychic protection issues can be solved with physical plane tools. It is always wise to use the appropriate tool for the job, and in this case, if you are dealing with emotional issues and situations, then approaching them from an emotional or mental perspective is the best way to go. This is one of the most sensitive, if not *the* most sensitive topic, and thus the potential is the highest for the greatest damage. There is a general tendency to throw the baby out with the bath water, so to speak, when it comes to emotions in general, so this can be a smorgasbord for energy vampires in one's life.

We'll start off by discussing the science behind this chapter. This really wasn't too much of a concern in the previous chapter other than providing the Latin names and discussing the fact there are warnings that should be considered, but in this chapter there is a little more to discuss before we move on to techniques. First of all, remember that the human body is seventy to seventy-five percent water. This is one of the reasons the phases of the moon have an effect on us. The principle is the same as the effect of the moon on the tides. Just as the moon exerts a pull on the tides, it exerts a pull on us as well. This is worth mentioning up front because one of the first ways to protect yourself emotionally is to know and be aware of the cycles of the moon. By themselves, these cycles can tell us the ambient energy in the air. It has been proven over centuries, time and again, that the Moon has a direct impact on the human form, if for no other reason than the fact that humans are seventy percent water, and it is a well-known scientific fact that the cycles of the Moon affect the tides, and thus, water in general. On a deeper level, these cycles can specifically affect people based on their astrological makeup. For example, if someone is born on a full moon, they will be affected by the full and new moons in different ways than others, and often these ways are stronger, with particular characteristics.

Also keep in mind that in the Western Esoteric Tradition, the element of water corresponds to emotions and the ability to move between the planes. Part of this also entails spirituality, in particular spiritual initiation. We can thus see how this is an appropriate correspondence: water to emotions. One of the ways this applies to the purpose of this text is that whenever you encounter emotional body issues, you can always focus upon your own personal and spiritual development as a major way to handle them.

Here I would like to interject some thoughts, and while they will point you in the direction of professional emotional support, this is not meant as a complete dissertation. Let's say someone is going through an emotional rough patch, such as a romantic breakup. Then, on top of it, they get fired from their job. To a casual observer, this may seem like a psychic attack, but it is simply a case of projection and cause and effect. Another part of this to consider is that you may not be necessarily getting psychically attacked, but rather going through a spiritual initiation of some sort. It is easy to confuse the two. An extension of this is that instead of being psychically attacked, perhaps you are going through a spiritual test of some sort. The twelve laws of karma I discussed in my book *Vocal Magick* are some of the ones I am referring to here, but there are many more universal, spiritual, and natural laws that may be coming into play. An example of a physical law that might seem like a psychic attack is that the biology of the human body changes through the years. This includes stages like puberty, the fact that the human brain doesn't fully develop until the mid-twenties, and the biological changes that happen after one turns forty. It can also relate to someone experiencing some sort of traumatic experience in their life, or even latent DNA that becomes activated through various means, such as when a person gets exposed to the triggers that activate them. Changes of life may seem like psychic attacks, when in reality they are natural processes. Learning about the human condition, physically, emotionally, and mentally, is invaluable when it comes to protecting yourself. This is one of the reasons why it is always wise to pay attention to science and what is continually being learned about the human condition and our physical bodies. Anyway, enough of the foundation. Let's turn our attention to more specific matters.

Maturity and Responsibility

The title of this section alone reveals one of the most if not *the* most important way you can psychically protect yourself when it comes to emotions. The tricky part of this is that how you do this is subjective, only applicable to *your* path, and where you are at when it comes to personal and spiritual development. So, while I can give you insights, advice, and tips, it still ultimately comes down to what works for you. We will break each one of these topics down and explore them in depth to create a baseline for ideas we will talk about later in the book. Let's start with maturity.

What maturity means to you is different than what it will mean to me, but let's start with the dictionary definition to establish a common point for reference. Unfortunately, the Oxford simply defines it as "The state, fact, or period of being mature." So, let's turn our attention to what mature means. The Oxford tells us the definition of mature is "fully developed physically; full-grown." The second definition is much more in line with our focus here: "(especially of a young person) having reached a stage of mental or emotional development characteristics of an adult." Thus, when we talk about emotional maturity, we are discussing handling and protecting one's emotions as an adult rather than as a child. While this may seem like common sense, I think we all know people that have problems with this, so it does bear mentioning here.

One of the meanings of maturity, in context of what we're discussing here, is that as we grow and evolve, we should learn to handle our emotions in better ways. The temper tantrums we threw as children to get our way should not be employed as we become adults, yet the vast majority of people still do throw fits, and often it works, because they are not told "no". If you are practicing psychic protection, handling your emotions in positive and mature ways protects you from those who seek to manipulate you emotionally. Many people gain energy from you if they rile up your emotions. They may not be aware they are siphoning off your energy, but they are doing it none the less. The trick here, though, is to realize that if you can't figure out how to handle your emotions in mature and healthy ways, then it is on you to find someone who can teach you, and there is a whole professional field dedicated to this. Therapists and counselors can be of great assistance, and while a great many people do seek them

Psychic Protection

out, a vast majority do not. One of the reasons for this is the stigma that is attached to this kind of therapy. People have a tendency to look down on others who seek assistance for handling emotions, yet ironically, they too should be in counseling, more often than not.

Everyone has emotional baggage. Most people in society today have experienced some sort of emotional trauma in their lives, and this is worth keeping in mind because it removes the stigma from seeking therapy. It is quite healthy to admit to yourself and to others that you are emotionally wounded and need help. Not only is it a sign of spiritual and personal growth, it is also the responsible thing for you to do, not only for yourself, but your loved ones, the planet at large, and the species as a whole. When we heal our emotional wounds, we take back our personal power that was lost at the time of the wound. In so doing, we increase our ability to achieve our goals and contribute to the overall growth of the human species. This also reinforces why we should treat others with compassion and understanding. Most people are reacting to things that occur from an emotionally wounded space, and while they may not be aware of it, this does not diminish this truth. It is easier to be in charge of your reaction to people and situations if you keep this in mind, because you are approaching the situation from a higher ground.

Often we can find sublime spiritual and occult truths in other areas of life, and in this case, we find an important occult lesson in martial arts. One of the common teachings in the swordplay of various cultures is that of the necessity of having the higher ground as a strategical advantage. Depending on the path you study, you will find various reasons and explanations for this. Particularly relevant to the purposes of this text are:

1) If you have the high ground, you have the advantage of better sight.

2) in the area of occultism, having the high ground

means being on the plane above the one you are engaging. When it comes to dealing with emotions, the high ground is the mental plane. By being firmly rooted in the mental plane, you are in complete control of your emotions. In other words, you are doing the emotions and not letting them do you.

This is no easy task, though, as you may assume. It is extremely difficult to reign in your emotions in the name of mental clarity and personal self-control. A side effect of this is that other people may see you as emotionally cold, detached, and distanced. While on one hand this may be true, it is only because it is necessary at that time. Keep in mind that just because others perceive this, it doesn't make it true. As a general rule of thumb, people fear and do not like what they don't understand. This doesn't mean having no emotions at all, for that is actually quite psychotic. Rather, it means exercising emotional control to the degree you can do what needs to be done at that time, in the appropriate way. A good axiom to remember is that "courage is resistance to fear, mastery of fear, not absence of fear." (Mark Twain) There are two helpful points to remember to help us accomplish this. First, the person who gets an emotional response from you controls you, and second, emotions are food, and therefore you are effectively starving your opponent. We'll speak more about this in a moment, but for now it should be clear. Let us shift gears to discuss emotional responsibility.

Emotional responsibility is something that is a little more difficult to understand, because part of it entails taking responsibility for your actions and emotions. This means honoring yourself as well as the emotions of others. For example, if someone says something to make you angry, it is responsible to tell them that, but not to throw a temper tantrum. Another point to keep in mind is to take the emotions of others into account when making major decisions that may impact them. This doesn't mean changing your decision so that they are not hurt. Rather, it means knowing that what you are deciding may affect them emotionally, and therefore you are responsible for how you engage with them when it comes to discussing the matter. There is a fine line here, though, which is that while you should be aware of how your decisions may emotionally impact others, this does not mean you are responsible for their emotions. The way to handle this is through your delivery and conversation with them.

Another part of emotional responsibility lies in honoring yourself, as mentioned above. Yes, you may be angry about something, but how do you vent that anger? That is the true test. Let's look at this from a more scientific perspective. When our emotions get triggered, certain chemicals are released in the body. These chemicals vary, depending on the emotions involved. Some of the chemical reactions also entail the release of adrenaline. Now knowing this, what do you do? The easy solution is to engage in some sort of activity that allows you to vent not only your emotions, but also those built up chemicals. I always like to joke with people that when I am the most upset, my place gets cleaned the most! I often use cleaning as a way to discharge those chemicals so that they don't stay imprisoned in the body. If you let those chemicals build up, they have been proven to lead to health issues down the road, especially if this is done over extended years. Much has been written about this, both metaphysically and physically, so there is plenty of further material available. By venting the chemicals as they build up, you keep your body closer to clean and pure than if you let them build up. This is one example of honoring yourself and handling your emotions in a healthy way. As another example, some people discharge their feelings by going through a workout at a gym with a personal trainer. No matter what you do, remember to engage in something that is productive rather than destructive. This is not only more satisfying, it is also safer. Part of the way this plays out is that by the time you are done venting those chemicals, there may not be enough energy left to have an emotional reaction to the situation. And, if you find that there *is* energy left for that, then engage in some other form of physical activity to vent the rest of it. Continue to do that until you are exhausted. Then, after the chemicals are vented, rest. One of the best phrases of wisdom I learned early in life is to "sleep on it." This means getting a full night's rest before making a decision or a plan. Not only does this recharge the body, it also gives you a chance to step back mentally and look at things from a fresh perspective. And if you should wake up feeling just as upset as you were the day before, then guess what? Yep, get back to the physical activity until you are exhausted. Repeat this cycle for as long as it takes.

Sometimes, though, we do not have the benefit of time that allows us to do this. In these instances, it is wise to keep a lock on our emotions, and to observe the chemicals running through our body rather than engaging in them. This is an idea that has been thoroughly discussed in various Buddhist teachings over the years, so you may find it helpful to look in that direction for further guidance. If you do temporarily turn off the emotions to focus on the task at hand, just remember to come back to dealing with them when you have the opportunity. If you find you cannot make time to do this, then introspection would be good to do, to see what subconscious block prevents you from loving and honoring yourself. One of the big reasons for this is that you may run the risk of living in denial of your emotions, and that could be more damaging down the road, not only to your health, but to the health of others. Not developing the ability to process emotions as an adult can lead not only to health issues, but also addiction problems and violent outbursts.

Astral Imprints

Now we turn our attention to the metaphysical side of the equation, but before we do that, we should lay some groundwork. Let's examine the astral plane. It is the closest plane to the physical, and encompasses the realms of emotions, desires, and basically all subjects related to raw, primal emotions. In Jungian terms, it is the alchemical imagination. It is where our desires create what we perceive, and this plane is the gateway between the world we live in and the upper worlds. In this way, the astral plane acts like a bridge. It's interesting that this bridge is built on desires and the imagination. There is an objective astral plane, too, and through the centuries this has been the meeting place of many adepts of various cultures and spiritual traditions. If you can conceive it, it exists on the astral plane, the realm of horror and splendor.

It is in this astral realm that we find valuable information about psychic protection, for people subconsciously and consciously have desires all the time. The astral plane can best be understood as being a gel or viscous fluid. It is malleable, but it can also be sticky and almost solid in some ways. Its fuel is the energy of the emotions. An easy formula to use to understand this is that energy follows thought, and thought begets form. The more emotions you pour into a situation or location, the denser and more palpable you make it. This is true of not only memories, but also physical locations. In other words, the more a particular spot witnesses repeated emotionally charged situations, the more it is imprinted with the general vibe and nature of those situations. For example, a place that is constantly home to people who have fits of rage, the more those locations are charged with a rage-filled energy.

A good example of this is in an urban setting, but the principles can apply anywhere. Let's say there is a tavern at 221B Baker St. And let's say that it has commonly been home to its fair share of bar brawls. Let's even say that it got so bad that eventually the tavern had to close. And, continuing the illustration, let's say that a new business, an apartment building, went up on its location. The astral imprint of the physical location being a place of debauchery, anger, and sorrow continues, even though the physical form is long gone. It would manifest in the way of attracting tenants that have those characteristics. Thus, even though the original purpose of the building has changed, the same kind of people might still frequent the location. So while the tavern is no longer there to encourage the same rage-filled behavior, it may be reported by various people in the apartment building. I hope this is a clear example of how the astral plane gets imprinted by repetitive actions fueled by emotions. This is also one of the reasons that holy sites will retain their potency, even if the dominant religion changes.

Another part of the equation is that this idea can be extrapolated to include the fourth dimension, that of time. This tells us that the longer a particular physical location is subjected to particular emotional experiences, the stronger it becomes, and the longer it will remain that way, almost regardless of future influences. This is the reason why holy places that are thousands of years old are still strong to this day. And of course, the greater the number of people who invest in its strength, the stronger it will become, and the longer lasting, too. This concept is tied into a larger paradigm that consists of thoughtforms and egregores, and while egregores are outside the scope of this book, thoughtforms are right in line with emotional health.

Thoughtforms

Truth be told, the term "thoughtforms" is a fairly new invention and has only been around for approximately 115 years or so. The book *Thoughtforms* by Annie Besant and C.W. Leadbeater was initially published in 1905, and while articles appeared in the magazine *Lucifer* before that, the term and concept weren't used much before the late 1800s at the earliest.

Thoughtform is a Western term adopted by the Theosophical Society that describes a far older concept: that of the "tulpa." References to this concept can be found in the Buddhist text *Samannaphala Sutta*, which is one of the earlier Buddhist texts, so we can get a rough idea of the time of its creation (a few centuries before Christ. Approximately 600 years BCE). In Buddhism, a tulpa is a being created through the concentration of psychic or mental energy.

As we can see, the way this applies to our text is that by knowing this, we now understand that the energy that is pooled on the astral plane in certain places can develop a level of sentience due to the energy generated by the same vibration of people over time. Using the aforementioned example of a tavern that no longer exists, we see that the consciousness of the thoughtform located there would have a consciousness produced by the type of people who frequented the establishment. So, the consciousness of the thoughtform would include the very primitive, base level traits of the alcoholic. If a proportion of the regulars were experiencing problems at home, then the thoughtform would also hold emotional baggage as part of its mentality. Further traits might include anger and extreme moodiness. Hopefully, it is clear where I am going with this.

Understanding this is important, because it reveals the level of consciousness vibration possessed by the thoughtform. Once you're aware of its consciousness level, you'll know what you can do about it. If you find yourself visiting places such as this, you should remember that maintaining a sense of logic, sobriety, and stable emotions can help protect you while you are there. If you do not protect your energy in such a location, you run the risk of gaining a lower astral attachment that may follow you home, and either begin to influence you in the name of survival, or simply catch a ride with you until it finds a more suitable host. In much the same way school children transmit diseases by bringing them home, thoughtforms can transmit themselves to the best vibratory fit for their survival. This also means you can create thoughtforms through conscious effort, but that is a conversation for another book.

Many times, the sources of psychic attacks may be energetic thoughtforms rather than flesh and blood people. There have been occasions in my life when I've had to cleanse myself energetically after being in such a stained location, and having picked up a particular thoughtform that was using me to get to its next meal, or worse yet, thinking *I* was its next meal! Basic banishings and cleansings will generally take care of these situations, and it is worth noting that this also means the more regularly we do our cleansings, the less impacted we are by these insidious beings.

Not all thoughtforms are negative, though. Consider a thoughtform of a local church that is known for its strength of faith. This could be a positive thoughtform that could manifest through someone who begins regularly attending services there, and their life turns around for the positive. Does this ring a bell or sound familiar to you? When you seriously consider and work with thoughtforms, you can see that they are the root of all gods and goddesses everywhere! Of course, this statement is based on the premise that we created the gods. We did, didn't we? Anywho...

Sometimes what we perceive as a psychic attack is actually an interaction with a thoughtform. Continuing the above story, let's discuss this for a moment. In the case of the churchgoing lady, she has come out ahead in life. The energetically sensitive person may have thought they were under psychic attack if they frequented the tavern mentioned above, but in reality they simply picked up on a thoughtform that was trying to survive. Yes, that could be considered an attack, or you could look at it as a primitive beast trying to devour what it needs to in order to survive.

One of the reasons for knowing all of this information is so that you will be in a better position to not only take care of your energy based on where you may find yourself in life, but also so that you can spot this in friends and loved ones. It also helps reinforce why we should perform regular energetic cleansings and banishings. People can accidentally create thoughtforms, especially around their own home or place of employment, and not realize it. By knowing how all of this works, we are more empowered and have a great tool of creation at our disposal.

Being aware of thoughtforms also reinforces why it is important to have emotional control. The strongest energy out there is that of emotions, and thus we see that the thoughtforms built through strong emotions – even those that are out of control – are the ones that are the strongest, but also the most primitive in their manifestation. By primitive, I mean that they are pure – concentrated and focused to the point that they appear singular in nature, when in reality they are simply focused. Underestimating thoughtforms is dangerous, so it is wise to tread lightly and carefully when dealing with them. To a lot of nonphysical entities, emotions are food, after all.

Points to Consider

When facing emotional situations, there are some valuable points to keep in mind to make empowered decisions that also protect your emotional body. There is much more advice available on this topic than the points discussed here, and there are plenty of books on the subject of emotional health, so if any of these strike a chord with you, you may want to consider investigating and researching them independently from the concept of psychic protection. There are also many health care professionals out there who are better equipped to help you if any of these are reoccurring themes in your life. The points discussed here are intended simply to stimulate your thought processes with regards to what it really means to protect yourself emotionally.

A good point to keep in mind when dealing with emotional situations is to "hold tightly, let go lightly." This is a reminder to live in the moment and be able to detach almost as quickly. You can see why it is great in principle, but of course implementing it is not so easy. Many people struggle with this throughout their lives, which means it is understandable if you struggle with it. While it is an excellent perch to attain, actually getting there is another story, and usually it is complicated by the fact it is a sliding scale of grey. You may go back and forth on this in various aspects of your life over the course of your life, and that is quite natural. However, by striving towards emotional control, we are constantly improving ourselves.

There are many thought and behavior patterns to watch out for, and by being aware of them, you are further protecting yourself psychically in a proactive way. The first thought pattern or behavior to address is fairly common: "If you really loved me, you'd do *x*." This is an unhealthy view to take, because love should not be demanding. This is known as emotional manipulation or emotional blackmail.

A trait to avoid when in romantic relationships is to rely on the other person to provide your happiness. This can be very dangerous leading to codependent relationships. Each person is responsible for their own happiness, which means it is on them to produce it when appropriate. While we can sympathize and even empathize with another, we should not put the power outside of ourselves when it comes to producing happiness in life. If our loved ones are down and depressed, then by all rights it is quite healthy to be down and in the dumps with them. This does have limits, though, and while the limits are subjective to each person, the overall concept is the same for all. Allow yourself to connect with your loved ones through sympathizing or empathizing with them but be careful not to take on those emotions as your own. An empath, particularly a natural one, may take on the depression of others to their own suffering and detriment.

Another good policy is to follow your heart, but lead with your head. Yes, follow your heart. However, apply logic, reason, and rationale to the situation, and use them to approach situations from a clear position. If you are the only one who uses this technique, then you might end up having to deal with other people's emotions and situations. Most likely this may manifest in a dramatic fashion. For example, if your heart says, "move across the continent," applying your head to the situation would tell you to figure out a plan on how to do it, rather than just picking up and moving without a plan. This also hints at the bigger picture, which is that the heart and brain are not mutually exclusive, but rather you should work with them together in a healthy fashion to achieve fulfilling success in all of life.

Expectations are something to avoid as well. Thinking things like "I know they'll change," when it comes to your loved ones, should be avoided. If they want to change, they will make it known and will actually do the work. On one hand, beware of blind faith, but on the other, it is all about making sure you see all emotionally charged situations clearly in life. This is also a warning against making excuses for the behavior of others. A line of thought here is "I'll let this slight go because I *know* they'll change their behavior." If appropriate, then yes, this is a healthy line of thought, but if you continue to say that to yourself, it might become an excuse you tell yourself instead of dealing with the problem, which is of course the other person or people involved in the situation you are pondering.

You should also watch out for abusive addictive relationships, as they can be insidious, forming from seemingly nothing into something huge to handle. These relationships might begin as an intense, passionate natural connection, only to turn into something that needs itself in order to survive. In other words, it becomes addictive. There is a serpent in paradise, and that is abuse, for because such relationships *are* so passionate and active, they may manifest as abusive, depending on the individuals involved. If the relationship ends up this way, both partners become addicted to each other, so neither leaves, the real issues never come up to be addressed and get swept under the rug, and the same pattern repeats. The true tragedy of these relationships is that there is a world of passion present, but little to no guidance, so things explode rather than evolve. I could go on and on about this, but I'll stop here for now.

The universal law of diminished returns must also be kept in mind. If you find you are putting more into the relationship than you could possibly get out of it over its duration, then it is wise to cut your losses and leave. This universal law teaches us discernment. If situations are lopsided, then there is no equality, rationale, etc. There is simply one ego conquering the other, which is okay if it was agreed upon from the start, but in most relationships this happens slowly rather than being planned. Universal laws are a subject that is not clearly understood by many people, and while the concept gets quoted a lot, they are very rarely discussed in depth, but they are important nonetheless. There are many of them, and even more are being discovered every day as we evolve as a species, which means more will be forthcoming in the future development of humanity. As we spiritually evolve, we open ourselves to being receptive to much more being brought to our awareness.

Having healthy boundaries and clear intent with people helps protect your emotional self, too. Regarding most situations in life, if you are in a position to put boundaries in at the beginning of a relationship rather than later, this is a wise move to consider. It is always easier to lay down boundaries early on but adding them in later can be emotionally sticky. You might find this technique helps you move forward, rather than if you apply it an existing, long-term relationship in your life. However, if you think you can heal a longstanding relationship by applying this idea, then go for it, and more power to you. A tangent of this is to have clear intent in all that you do. Not only does this warn against muddled energy that can be transmitted by having divided attention, it also reminds you that there is strength in purity, and that strength is formidable when used appropriately.

A powerful perception to keep in mind when you are interacting with people on a day to day basis is that everyone is doing the best they can with the tools at their disposal. This can be a hard lesson to learn, because it teaches you that you shouldn't get angry with people who don't live up to your expectations. Accepting that the decisions other people make on any given day are the best decisions they *can* make takes a lot of courage and strength. It also requires humility and acceptance. While you might think it's sad that those are the only tools such people have at their disposal, it should still be accepted without judgement.

A valuable question to ask yourself when it comes to many emotional situations is "What's the point?" This hints at perspective and reminds you to keep everything in clear context of the greater whole. Sometimes, if you're not careful, you might blow situations out of proportion in your mind and make mountains out of mole hills. This lesson warns against that. It also tells you that through working with this material on a regular basis, you'll see that sometimes you *are* disappointed with the behavior of others but, keeping the lesson in mind, do you really have a right to be?

As you can see, the central theme of this chapter is emotional control, and also being aware that sometimes we have to call in professionals who work with these situations on a regular basis. If any such situations are occurring in your life, you may want to seek help from qualified professionals. Keep these ideas in mind when you are evaluating and addressing situations in your life concerned with emotions and emotional charges. Remember that many beings feed off the raw energy that we all emit on any given day. Their activity and attention to us may appear falsely as psychic attacks, when in reality there are other causes, such as psychological and emotional issues, (as addressed above), or perhaps a lower vibrational thoughtform scrounging for sustenance. It is wise to keep these things in mind during assessment of what is happening in your life. This can save a lot of headaches later down the road. It can also help develop your clairvoyant skills as you look at things magically throughout your life. By keeping to the principles discussed here, you are in a greater position of empowerment through the entirety of your life. When in doubt, remember to control the emotions and not let them control you.

Chapter Six
Vampires

Originally, I was going to talk about boundaries in this chapter, but instead of treating the symptom, let's treat the cause and look at the underlying energetic. Let's discuss vampirism.

You can tell by the context that we're not going to be discussing the classic folk character that drinks blood and could really use some vitamin D. We are going to focus on energetic and emotional vampires specifically, as they are the ones that will most likely be encountered in day to day life. They are the vampires that can do the most damage to a person and their life. We can't just discuss them in a broad swath approach though, as there are many different kinds of vampires, and not all are bad. I have known many in my life who are good people I enjoy spending time with, but by that same token, I have known many who were horrible people, moving in and destroying lives like professionals. This broad spectrum of types of vampires explains why there are so many misconceptions in both the modern spiritual movement, and outside of it, as to what vampirism actually is, and its visage to the general public.

As we take a closer look at the subject, we should remember that at the end of the day, almost everyone has experienced a certain level of vampirism, either engaging in it or being victimized by it, so to pass any blank judgment on the subject or particular people you may know or meet, would be a naïve exercise in morality. Like most things in life, situations you may encounter should be viewed subjectively, in that each one is unique and teaches a different lesson, even though it may resemble situations from your past. Often, spiritual lessons that were not learned the first time will come back around to be dealt with in a different way, and sometimes a lesson is more complex than it first appears, so there is more to be learned than what can be packed into a singular experience.

The vampire subculture that consists of dress, culture, and the exchange of blood on a consensual basis is outside the range of this book. We will specifically be looking at emotional and psychic vampires, because they are generally the ones you may have to protect yourself against. These people are the ones who feed off emotions or the psychic energy of others, either subconsciously or knowingly. Vampirism, as it relates to this book, is when one takes something from another living being in order to feel healthy or fulfilled. To a certain extent, everyone has experienced this. Think back to a time in your life when you were enjoying time with friends, and after you left their presence, you still felt that particular joy. Sometimes this may manifest as feeling energetically drunk, as in the buzz generated from a massive release of psychic energy and emotions. This is worth remembering because it reminds us to be compassionate when appropriate.

Different Types of Vampires

Before we move onto metaphysics, let's talk about the accompanying psychology that is necessary to note to emotionally protect yourself. Functionally, there are two types of vampires: Knowing ones, and those who are engaging in the practice, blissfully unaware of what they are doing. Each one requires a different approach, so be aware that this is a case where a blanket response is best avoided. Once we discuss these two perspectives, we will move onto the next level.

People who engage in vampirism fully aware of what

they are doing can again be split into two categories: people who do so ethically, and those who don't. It is easy to know which side of the fence someone is, though, because the ethically inclined will not practice vampirism upon someone so *without permission!* So the various combinations of these are knowing vampires who are ethical, and those who are not.

Those who practice vampirism knowingly and ethically are some of the more interesting and intelligent people I have had the pleasure of knowing. They are generally full of life and enjoy the pleasures of the world and the flesh, and can thus be good people to talk to if you have a dilemma that could negatively impact your enjoyment of incarnation. If they want your emotional or psychic energy, they will ask and discuss it with you. This also makes them some of the most polite people you may meet. On average, these people are safe from an emotional perspective. Of course, there are jerks in all groups, so you may encounter a rogue jerk, but that is true of all groups in society.

However, those who do it knowingly and unethically are those who have bred negative stereotypes that most people in society know and do not like. These are the people who will take your energy without asking for permission, which could leave you feeling drained after being in their presence. They take and give nothing in return, completely disrespecting you in the process. These people can be hard to spot, as they generally do their best to conceal their agenda. However, this also makes them a cautionary tale for those who think there is no value in emotional boundaries or daily cleansings and banishings.

There is another side to the equation, though, and this addresses what the true danger is in day to day life. What we are talking about here are those who do not know they are psychic vampires yet affect people negatively without realizing it. These are the people who will do their best to get an emotional rise out of you, because on some level it feeds them. In some cases, this is a medical condition that can be addressed and, as I'm sure you've figured out, it can also be a treatable mental condition. There are those who are fully aware and conscious of what they're doing, and those are who we're talking about here. This hammers the point home, I'm sure. This is why it is always smart to project emotional boundaries as a normal practice, and to make sure you handle your emotions carefully and healthily as a natural state of being.

Knowing, Ethical Vampires

I have known many of this type over the years, and they can be some of the more interesting and nicest people you'll meet in the occult community. They tend generally have an interesting fashion sense, and actually know what they're talking about when it comes to all things related to vampires. Many of them feed psychically in some sort of mutual exchange with people over the course of their life. Some even take it a step further and exchange actual blood. Like many communities out there, it has its share of problem people, but for the most part they are as uncommon in ratio as any other subcommunity in society.

They have their own code of ethics but, as I don't spend enough time in that culture to know the nuances of said ethical code, I won't try to talk about that here. From what I have experienced, it is in line with an honor code from an honorable person in general. They are also generally very good at working with and embracing consent culture, which is always a nice thing to see! They, like many other people in various occult communities, simply like to follow their spiritual path without interruption, and some of the gnosis they have brought to occultism is very interesting, to say the least.

Knowing, Unethical Vampires

As hinted at above, these are vampires who can be particularly troublesome, because at their very core they are largely narcissists. They are driven by their reptilian brain, believing in sensory gratification, and the more immediate, the better. They truly feed off the energy they obtain from others, and this is often the energy generated by strong emotions. Some feed on the natural psychic energy a person emits, but no matter the type of energy, it is still sustenance acquired from an outside source. Sometimes this need to feed is a subtle manifestation of internal chemical imbalances, so in some cases, this deficiency can be remedied with medical treatment. Not all go that way though, and many choose to turn it into part of their spiritual path in some way. The interesting thing about this group is that they may not be interested in the occult or spiritual at all. This is what makes them truly dangerous. This also tells us that there is often something wrong with them psychologically.

When they take that energy from others, it fills a void within the self. Forgetting the Hermetic axiom, they often become disempowered, believing they are a victim of circumstances outside of their control, when in reality they are choosing not to look within in the first place. If they're not careful, they could also become addicted to this sort of behavior, making their condition worse. They are often very nice and sociable people, but there are most likely emotional or psychological issues that go with their condition. This underscores the need for patience and also that you should take time to get to know people in general as a good emotional health defense mechanism. Remember that to the mature mind, trust is earned, and never given freely. It is not so much that there is a defensive agenda being advanced, but rather that you are working in an ongoing way with the principles of the planet Saturn to achieve success throughout life. Saturn is the planet of maturity, foundation, structure, discipline, karma, and being grounded.

Unknowing, Unethical Vampires

There's not a lot more I can add here that wasn't discussed in the previous section, but there are a few points I can make for clarity. Th behavior of this type is more or less the same, or similar to, that of the knowing unethical vampire, but they are simply unaware of the whole process. In this way they are usually drama kings or queens, causing commotion in their lives from which to feed, and then wondering why drama never leaves them alone. Many times, they are emotional manipulators, which of course underscores the importance of working with the traits of Saturn.

A certain level of compassion and care should be taken when dealing with this type, though. First of all, if you know someone like this, and you think you can help them address the matter for their own benefit, the first thing to do is to seek out the appropriate health care professional. See if your concerns are grounded or not, because sometimes what we see in others is what is internally occurring within ourselves that needs to be addressed.

Not everyone can handle being told they are a vampire of any kind, which is why compassion and care should be kept in mind. Make sure the other person can handle the conversation. Think very carefully before bringing this topic up because relationships can end or take a turn for the worse if this isn't handled delicately. In most cases, tenderness can assuage this kind of conversation, so make sure you know the person very, very well before engaging in a discussion. Remember that the point of the conversation is for their healing. For example, you can approach the conversation from the perspective of: "This is

Psychic Protection

what I'm seeing. Is it true?" Or, "I've seen some traits you have that raise red flags, and I want to know if I'm seeing things clearly."

Non-Physical Vampires

Previously we discussed thoughtforms and psychic stains that can be left in particular places, and the sentience that goes with them, but let's add to that conversation. Some beings you may encounter through your development might not be physical and will not fall into the category described in the previous chapter. The initial beings that come to mind are demons and other malevolent entities that are common themes for the plots of stories centuries old. The succubus and incubus come to mind at first thought, and with a few moments of reflection, I'm sure plenty of others will come to your mind, too. These very very old thoughtforms have attained a degree of consciousness that no human can fathom. How can I say that with certainty? Well, we have physical limits and the limits that come with being in physical form. We also do not have access to all of the memories of the part of us that extends beyond just this one life. The beings mentioned above are not confined by either of these restrictions, and therefore possess an unbroken consciousness dating from the first recording of their type and/or name until now. All we know of ourselves is what we remember from this life, and what knowledge we have gleaned from spiritual development about the memories of other lives.

A strong warning comes up here that should be kept in mind when dealing with spirits of all kinds. While we may be able to relate and interact with them, we cannot fool ourselves into thinking that we know their minds. Consider this, though: 90 percent of the time people interact with spirits successfully, so while this sounds scary due to its alien nature and nebulous nature, it really isn't, as long as you follow the protocols for spirit communication that works for them in their spiritual growth. This lesson warns against hubris, which has been the downfall of many a good magician over the centuries. These beings have their own agendas, perceptions, and mental strengths and weaknesses, just like we do.

If an entity is vampiric in nature, this tells us they have many different ways to drain our energy, and even if we sat around and thought about this for a long time, we could not figure out all of their methods, nor should we even try, really. If we deal with them, then, it is on us to treat them respectfully and fairly. As long as we do that, interaction should generally go smoothly. Here again, though, this largely depends on what we learned about the being before choosing to work with them. The value of knowing correspondences cannot be understated, as we learn about their psyches so that we can manifest positive results. We learn their tastes, their peculiarities, and their abilities, and thus we know how to relate to them. Funny enough, this brings us full circle to the intelligent application of boundaries.

For the most part, these beings are not confined to any particular place, unlike the thoughtforms discussed previously, but some are stronger in certain places than others. Usually these are the places in which they were born and are commonly found upon our research. And, many times, they are just one of a number of spirits that share the same characteristics, so there are many out there in the world at large. Consider the fact that many different cultures and civilizations believe in beings with similar correspondences, only differing by name. You can see that running into these beings can be quite common even if you go through life unconsciously. By adjusting your vibration, these beings are easily shed, but it does take an indefinite time to solidify the higher vibration. After this occurs, the vampiric being cannot find a connection to the occultist, and thus usually moves on to find another source of sustenance. After all, energy follows the path of least resistance throughout the cosmos. These rules drastically change when it comes to magicians, but that is a conversation for another time and place.

Avoiding Vampirism

To each their own when it comes to spiritual growth, as long as it is harming no one else, but this discussion does set the stage for the next part of this chapter. We can, and should, make sure we are healthy enough to avoid the pitfalls that can lead to vampirism if it would diminish our overall quality of life and spiritual ascent. You can see from the listed conditions that if you're not careful, there is actually a danger of becoming an unknowing vampire. So it is wise to concern yourself with making sure things are copacetic.

I hinted at this earlier, but let's expand it. What is it, you ask? The Hermetic Axiom. Attributed to being written by the Egyptian god Tehuti (Thoth) himself, this is one of the older pieces of spiritual wisdom over the centuries, and it simply states "That which is above is like that which is below, and that which is within is like that which is without." Or, something like that. Translations and interpretations vary, but this is the essence of it. We are the microcosms of a greater macrocosmic reality, and as we are internally, we are externally, too. Many cynics over the years have taken issue with this, but by and large, spiritually speaking, this is truth. If we feel like we have an internal void, we will try and fill it, consciously or not.

The way this applies to our conversation is as a reminder of why we should practice emotional health. A lot of things pertaining to emotional and spiritual fulfillment can be found within rather than without. If we think we need something without, we should first look within to see if we can fulfill that need ourselves. Sometimes this can be done through spiritual and psychological means, but other times we may find we have accidentally come across a chemical deficiency within ourselves. Or perhaps it is that we discovered a part of our psyche that needs some healing. In any event, I trust you see what I mean. We cannot always assume that the Hermetic axiom is always true. It does have its limits when it comes to biology and science but, for the most part, what we lack internally can be resolved by going within.

Through our emotional vigilance, we stay on top of our emotional, spiritual, and mental health. At the same time, we also sharpen our senses, not just for our own well-being, but also to see those around us who may need some healing. When we do this for long enough and thoroughly enough, we sharpen our psychic skills in the process. This makes it a win-win situation. it also puts us in a better position of greater personal empowerment when it comes to interacting with the average person in our daily lives. However, it also means that our psychic skills will grow on their own. This point is worth emphasizing because I have known people who have awakened or sharpened their psychic skills to the degree that they could then see spirits and energy when they couldn't before, and it caught them off guard. They didn't know this was a potential side effect and were therefore blindsided. Sometimes this resulted in them shutting down psychically, and in some cases they did or did not open them back up later. This is further proof that all of our bodies are connected (Physical, emotional, mental, and spiritual).

After we take a moment to reflect on everything we've digested in this section, we see that it is not so much about knowing a particular *reactionary* way to protect ourselves, but rather training ourselves to be able to spot the principles at work around us most of the time we are out and about in our daily lives. Being able to recognize what is going on around us, and our role within it, we further empower ourselves to achieve success and to protect what we have. This is the foundational cornerstone of this book: proactivity through perception. The best psychic protection you can have is knowledge, and the best response is to be in control of your actions. Remember when we discussed swordplay earlier? When it comes to dealing with emotions, the high ground is considered the mental plane, and being in control of one's emotions to deliver the appropriate response.

Emotional Responses

Continuing the deferral theme of "there are many books available devoted solely to this subject," this section will be fairly short and open to further exploration if something within it resonates with you. The same response is not always the appropriate one to a given situation, and this is a common rule for life.

Several years ago, a friend of mine told me something interesting before he died. He told me that when he was raising his children, he taught them to make appropriate decisions in addition to basic morality. In a lot of ways, this rearranged my thinking, moving the concept of appropriateness to a higher priority in my mind. Then I was able to connect the dots to another interesting piece of the puzzle. Something I learned from hypnotherapy many years ago was that the way a person responds emotionally to various stressful situations can tell us a lot about the level of their emotional maturity. The general line of thinking here is that if someone responds to an emotionally charged situation as an adult in a way that is immature, this reaction reveals at what age the person received such an emotional wound that they ceased to learn coping skills as they grew older from that age. For example, if you know someone who punches a wall every time they are emotionally upset, you can deduce that they experienced a major emotional trauma at a young age, usually under the age of five or six, specifically, because that is how a young child would react. Yes, this is a blanket concept, and it should be remembered there are exceptions to every rule, but by and large, if you keep this in mind when dealing with others and their emotions, you will find that you develop a better intuitive understanding of most people, and this can be helpful when you meet and interact with them in daily life.

The trick lies in doing your research to learn what ages could potentially cause particular reactions so that you know how to analyze what you experience. I can provide some basic ideas, but for more detailed information, seek out the appropriate material written by professionals in the field. Usually, if someone responds from a tantrum perspective as described above, this reveals that the emotional wound occurred when the individual was very young, and had not learned how to handle their emotions yet, so you could guess (and I emphasize 'guess') that the emotional trauma probably occurred before age six. A trick I use to evaluate this is to think back to my younger years when confronted with these kinds of situations. I think back to where I was mentally when I would have responded in that fashion. This narrows things down dramatically and puts me in a position of greater empowerment for when it is time for an appropriate response. This is one of the fruits of the Buddhist teaching that you should watch your thoughts flow through your mind like a river, yet never engage with them. While this may seem extremely abstract at the moment, we will be coming back to it in the next section when we turn our attention to the mental plane, so it is better to recognize the foundation being built here.

Another revealing response is found through astrology. If we know the basic elemental makeup of who we are

Psychic Protection

interacting with, we can have an idea of how to interact with them, and how to respond to them. This is an advanced thought to consider, but it is still important to note here.

Yet another point to keep in mind when evaluating someone's response is whether or not the person closes off emotionally. This doesn't necessarily reveal anything about the age at which they suffered an emotional wound, but it does reveal how the person processes (or not) emotions when they come up in life. Living in denial or suppressing emotions can be a toxic practice, and eventually can lead to physical damage, as recent studies have shown. Thus you gain insight into their emotional body and health, and this information can be used in the name of healing, or whatever response is appropriate.

So much of how to protect yourself emotionally can be found through consulting professionals in their respective fields, and I will not even attempt to match their expertise here. This illustrates the necessity of consulting the correct channels for greatest health. I could tell you about all kinds of emotional cleansings rituals, etc, but I see no reason to, because everyone has their own spiritual path with corresponding practices. Even though this is a smaller chapter, it discusses one of the largest, if not *the* largest area of our being that needs protection. This is good foundational material for growth, rather than meant as a be-all-end-all resource. More people have emotions than are into occultism, and therefore these themes will be dealt with in more places than occult scenarios and environments. Daunting as it may sound, this also makes it the greatest area of our lives for proactive healthy growth. While some may see all of this as defeating, it should also be considered as opportunistic. It is because of all of this that we can achieve tremendous emotional growth during this lifetime, and often this feeds directly into our spiritual growth overall.

Bill Duvendack

We now turn our attention to the next plane, the mental, and we should remind ourselves of the wisdom of Dion Fortune: "In order to have power over a plane, you must approach it from the plane above."

Section Three
Mental Plane Tools

Chapter Seven
Body Language and Hypnosis

We're now going to shift gears and rise to the mental plane, but before we do, there are a few preliminary points to discuss. The first relates to the order of the planes. The mental is higher than the emotional because it is the mind that is in control of the emotions in a healthy life. However, these planes overlap, and are not mutually exclusive. In other words, when we are engaging our emotions, our mental plane is also engaged, and when we are using our mind, our emotions are stirred. This line of thinking also applies to the physical and spiritual planes and has been discussed in many self-improvement books in recent years that address becoming emotionally invested in living a full and fulfilled life.

I have noticed through the years that there are two wide groups of people:

1) those who go through the motions in all that they do, never really emotionally connecting with what they're doing.

2) those who are emotionally invested in the processes of life. Generally, these people tend to get further than those who just go through their lives on autopilot, internally emotionally dead. By cultivating a good connection between the heart, mind, and spirit, one achieves health and success.

The mental plane is the realm of logic, reason, rationale, clear intent, focus, and discipline. At the higher end of the plane, it encompasses abstract thoughts, and at that point it begins to blend with the plane above it, the spiritual.

Most of what we will be discussing in this section will concern mental discipline, emotional detachment, and logic. However, remember, "Follow your heart, but lead with your head." This is the plane a lot of people have challenges with due to the amount of self-control and mental discipline it takes to achieve success. Part of the price you pay for being adept with the mental plane is being seen as emotionally cold or distant, removed from one's emotions. Over time, I have noticed though, that these people need support more than others because of the internal intensity they experience when working with this plane repeatedly. If you are not careful, you can lose your spiritual and emotional bearings, and become the cold hearted person you might have been accused of being for far too long. This withers and atrophies compassion and emotions in general, and I'm sure I don't need to tell you the various psychological issues that come with that.

So why would one develop mental plane skills, if these are the dangers? The most obvious answer is emotional control. A tangent of thought here is that often the people who are the most adept with the mental plane are natural empaths who have chosen the path of self-control and healing in the name of understanding their gifts and spiritual growth. Another benefit to developing these skills is that it puts you in a position to receive greater spiritual gnosis from higher vibrational beings the more you develop that skill set. By cultivating these skills, you also train your mind so that you have less reliance on tools overall. About that...

Do we need to use tools to accomplish our Will? Technically no, but boy, are they fun to use! Ultimately our mind is the ultimate tool, but this doesn't mean you should avoid using tools. Using tools creates muscle memory but are ultimately left behind when we die and continue our journey on the other side. I have met people who felt like they could do nothing without their tools, but I have also met people who don't use magical tools because of what we're talking about here. Remember that extremism in any case is wrong and unhealthy, so it is wise to come to your own conclusion regarding tools and to stick with it, changing it when necessary. By developing mental plane skills, you will come into an increased sense of awareness, which in turn will feed your spiritual growth.

Because of the cerebral nature of this plane, many of the techniques and tools we'll discuss will be more psychological in nature, which means that you can find more qualified professionals in their respective fields than I, and the same words of wisdom mentioned before apply here as well. We will once again touch upon broad concepts and subjects that you can use to protect yourself psychically, but to fill in the details it will take research and experience. I have found what we will talk about in here will also cross over into the spiritual realm, and yet remain in the mental plane, forming a bridge of sorts. When applied on a regular basis, this information can help train your mind to think in new ways and perceive things that others might miss. This means you will begin to separate from others, but this is a good thing, as it helps you attain new heights of spiritual progress. The mind is the ultimate tool, but that also means it takes the most work in a lot of regards. Thus this plane is not for the hobbyist and can lead to a new way of life, a new way of being. Let's break things down and get to the details.

Body Language

The ability to read body language cannot be emphasized enough when it comes to protecting your emotional body. If you had to pick one skill from this chapter to learn, this would be the one. Thankfully enough, this is also one subject that has been written about a lot over the last several decades and is in common use in more areas of society than just occultism, so there is a plethora of material available to the curious seeker. A great book to begin with is *The Naked Ape*, by Desmond Morris. It has been around for about fifty years and is a wonderful starting point.

In this book, the author, a human biologist, discusses the animalistic side of human nature, in particular how our bodies behave in social circles and situations. It is a great primer to understanding the animal side of our nature that so many modern spiritual thinkers and writers tend to ignore. Never forget that we are humans, but we are also half animal. It is wise to keep this in mind throughout life, because if we deny our animal side, we are only setting ourselves up for pain later in life. This suppression can fall into the same category of what we have previously discussed regarding the suppression of emotions. Neither one is good to do. We should engage in and deal with our emotions, and we should engage in and deal with our animal nature, too. The trick is to stay in control of how this happens. If we lose control, very bad things can happen, because our human side would be second in strength to our raw, primal, nature. This usually manifests as acts of violence, but there are many ways it can play out in life.

One of the perceptions Morris makes in his book gives us valuable insight into what we can expect from it, and also serves as an introduction to the kind of techniques that are effective on a mental level. Related concepts will be discussed in this chapter, but it is in no way a comprehensive or exhaustive list. It does serve as a starting point for our conversation and opens the door to a greater understanding of mental psychic protection. A technique from the book I found memorable and useful concerns people-watching, especially couples. If you are out and about in society and you see a couple who are obviously in a romantic relationship, watch them for a few seconds. Read their body language, but specifically look at where their hands and arms are. If they are an affectionate couple and hold hands, or even put their arms around each other, look to see where those arms fall. If they fall around the waist and seem to be more relaxed, then the odds are that they have had sex since their relationship began, whereas if the arms are tenser and located higher on the torso, then they probably haven't. I use this here as an example because it is a clear-cut example of what this book discusses, and what we are talking about when it comes to reading body language. Details and subtleties can provide a lot of insight into what a person is thinking and what their subconscious is telling you.

This works both ways, though, as knowledge of body language also puts you in the driver's seat to use those same techniques to protect yourself against anything that might come your way. Some of this information may be more common knowledge than other aspects of reading body language, and this simply enforces how common this knowledge is. Its value is almost unlimited, though, and studying the subject would definitely be worth your time. At least, I have found it worth my time, and have had success with the techniques we are discussing here. If you are aware and in control of your body language, you project that energy into the multiverse at large and this inherently raises your vibration. After all, the body is the subconscious mind. It is the microcosm to the macrocosm of the ascended self. I'm going to discuss techniques simply as they are and generally will leave the intent of their usage up to you, because many of them can be used proactively and reactively, so I see no reason to go into that level of detail. After all, it's a scientific method of thinking. If something is true, so is its converse, meaning if something can be used one way, it can also be used in an opposite way. Simply, this one piece of scientific wisdom can expedite spiritual and personal growth, and can assist in developing the consciousness in interesting and unique ways.

One of the most, if not *the* most commonly known technique of body language is that of crossing your arms across your chest when someone says something that triggers your defensiveness. If you are talking to someone and they do that, you probably hit a nerve or a hurdle of some kind. Remember common sense, though, and pay attention to your environment. If it is cold outside, then it is more than likely the chill that is causing the person to cross their arms rather than revealing any subconscious information. That idea applies to all body language information and techniques in general. The environment supersedes a revelation of a subconscious intent. Yes, many times they are hand in hand, but be careful not to mistake one for another. When we look at this technique energetically, we see that when someone crosses their arms across their chest, they are blocking their solar plexus chakra, the *manipura*, largely preventing energy from reaching it. If you do it, it accomplishes the same goal, and thus we can see how it is a defensive move.

It is harder for energy to lock onto you if you are constantly or almost constantly in motion. One of the ways you can use this knowledge is to constantly be in motion in some way, subtle or overt, when you are interacting with people. I use this technique a lot when I am doing public presentations, and I have seen other professional motivational speakers do it, too, so it is more common than you might think. Rocking back and forth, or at least being in movement when talking, can keep unwanted energy away from you. This is also a good way to keep your own circulation going.

Some situations might occur, however, when we are not in a position to do either of these techniques, so we may feel caught off guard. When surprising situations occur, there's not much we can do in the moment, but we can control our response. A technique I have found useful is that when the first opportunity avails itself, take it and excuse yourself to the bathroom. Wash your hands in water, and while you do so, visualize washing away all of the energy accumulated from the previous environment. With concentration, you may find this easier and easier to do through repetition, and it will leave you feeling pure and clean. There are other concepts and techniques like this that can be done, but they are all derivatives of this one. Some of these you can discover on your own through experimentation, but others you may find through research.

A technique I learned through spiritualism is also done when you are alone. Run your projecting arm down the front of your body in a sweeping motion, crossing your torso. While doing this, visualize that your arm is cutting energetic cords that may have attached themselves to your chakras and aura in general. Once you get comfortable with that technique, a tangent of that is to run your arm down your back as well, to achieve the same end. This is also a reminder that we should watch and cleanse our back, and that it is not all about the front of our bodies. Many times, this point gets glossed over or completely ignored in energy work, but it is of vital importance. What is true for the front of the body is generally also true for the back.

Body language is part of a greater paradigm that we can look to for further techniques to protect ourselves. This greater paradigm is that of consciously co-creating your daily reality in line with your Will and your vision for yourself. The most common and popular way to do this is not founded in mysticism or the occult, but rather through the power of your mind, hypnosis.

Hypnosis

Do you want to quack like a duck on a stage in front of people? If you do, then you can look into prestidigitation, (conjuring or stage magical tricks) or the siddhis of Eastern traditions (a variety of alleged supernatural powers). While a form of hypnosis is used in these practices, it is not the kind we are discussing here. We will look specifically at using hypnosis, and self-hypnosis, as a means of psychic protection. This technique is included here because a lot of it can frequently overlap with body language, and when the two are combined, they can achieve powerful results. This is true not only from a protection perspective, but also from a co-creative one, too. Hypnosis also points the finger in the direction of being proactive, so it can be a very empowering skill to learn. Good friends of mine are professional hypnotherapists from whom I have learned a lot over the years, and I wish to share a lot of their practices here. Again, seeking out the proper professionals in the field is the preferred way to go, but if you want a quick reference and brief tips, I will include them here.

Before discussing techniques though, there are some preliminary thoughts to share to create a common foundation. The first one I hinted at above, which is that the body is the subconscious mind. I realize a lot of people might not believe this, but more and more scientific research is revealing a mind/body connection that we are only beginning to understand and address, but the evidence demonstrates there is some sort of connection, regardless. As to the extent and power though, this is still highly subjective and open to interpretation. Bluntly, not enough research has been done to clarify this further at the time of writing, but the connection itself does exist, and has been proven. This tells us that the more we develop and train the mind, the more we gain control over our bodies. Conversely, we can also read our body to see what is going on in our subconscious.

We should cut this subject and information with Occam's Razor though and remind ourselves that sometimes what is going on with the body may not be reflective of the mind at all. This is easily analyzed when we stop to remind ourselves that we have genetic karma as much as we have energetic or spiritual karma. When we choose to incarnate, we do address karma that concerns being in physical form. A lot of times, this genetic karma relates to the family line and settling up family karma; it is not so much indicative of the subconscious as of what physical karma is being addressed. We should not assume that just because we read something in our body it is automatically a message from our subconscious. It may be a message regarding genetic karma.

    Another point to be aware of is that, on average, it takes twenty-eight days for the subconscious to learn a new behavioral pattern. I say on average because it depends on the pattern being addressed. If you have a deeply embedded behavioral pattern from childhood, it may take a lot longer than just twenty-eight days to address it, so patience is always encouraged when dealing with training the mind. You can also see that by my choice of words that modern psychology can also be consulted to gain further insight into what we are discussing here. And, as you may have suspected, psychology and hypnosis have more in common than differences, and people who are proficient in one are often proficient in, or at least knowledgeable about, the other, even if they don't practice it. I have known many hypnotists over the years, as well as those who learned it on their own, and all of them have an understanding of psychology as well. Knowing how the mind works, both physically and from a behavioral perspective, can be of great value when it comes to protecting your energy. Whether you use this information to protect yourself, or simply to be able to spot it when other people are using those techniques in your presence, it is still important to be aware of all aspects to keep your energy clear, and to give you another tool in your toolbox for the co-creation of your reality.

When you are embedding a new behavioral pattern in yourself, it will take at least twenty-eight days of sustained effort. This also teaches us a valuable esoteric lesson. It is better to focus on attracting what we want and play to our strengths, delegating our weakness. A good real-world example of this is that if you are against war, you don't go to an anti-war rally, but rather you attend a pro-peace rally. Energy flows where attention goes, after all. I covered this extensively in *Vocal Magick*, and you can reference that book for more information.

Esoterically speaking, this also removes the possibility of a polarity-based conflict. This matters because, remember, the key to success is in having the high ground, whether it is moral, mental over emotional, or simply in psychologically removing yourself from a polarity-based situation. There is a lot of energy generated through conflict, which can be harnessed and applied to various goals, but the more time and energy you spend in conflict, the more you will engage in a battle of wills, which rarely ends well. When protecting your energy, it's wise to remember you can choose to exit any sort of conflict you encounter. This doesn't mean you should; it also means that you shouldn't. Maintaining the high ground is important, but sometimes the energy of the conflict can be put to good use in producing larger than expected results for various projects in life.

In order to improve your mental armor, it is wise to learn this information and apply it at various periods in your life to achieve various goals. You can use this information to break bad habits you may have, to train bad behavior out of loved ones, and to be able to spot when such tactics are being used against you. An extension of this material is NLP, which is short for "Neuro-Linguistic Programming." In short, this is the incorporation of body language into traditional hypnotic techniques, and while it's a fairly new subject of study, it has really been around for quite a long time, as anyone who works in sales will tell you. This can further enhance your ability to defend yourself mentally.

A common way this is accomplished is through the popular technique of *affirmations*. These are brief sayings you can tell yourself in order to advance a particular way of thinking. Sometimes they are called mantras, but that is an inaccuracy, as mantras are specific to the Hindu tradition. The concept is the same, though. An example of an affirmation is "All I can handle for my greatest growth and good is brought to me at this time." The point of this affirmation would be to reinforce an optimistic and personal development thought pattern. Affirmations serve to affirm a particular way of thinking, so it is best to use those that enforce the positive. As you can see, affirmations are a form of self-hypnosis and this illustrates another way the mind can be manipulated. We will discuss how to use affirmations to achieve spiritual effects later, but since the concept is mental in nature and application, it does require discussion and introduction here.

By being proactive when it comes to addressing and training the mind, you put yourself in a position of protection, for it is the mind that is usually influenced or affected during psychic attacks. It is harder for the energy to get a foothold if the target has mentally trained their mind in various disciplines that we are discussing here. While we have touched on hypnosis, NLP, body language and affirmations, there are many other ways to train the mind. I don't claim to know all of them, but am familiar enough with the fact that there are many more out there I have not come across. Much of what we're discussing here relates to your creative problem-solving skills as much as with using logic and reason, as mentioned before.

It might seem counterintuitive to consider creative problem-solving in the context of this discussion, but it serves as a reminder that the higher part of the mental plane is abstract. This is where it also begins to blend with the spiritual plane. As much as we develop our logical and mental faculties, we should be mindful this doesn't become our prison, limiting our thinking. Yes, logic is good, but it is not an absolute solution. As mentioned before, living your life occurs upon a sliding scale of grey, rather than black and white extremes. This also includes how you handle protecting your energy. Approaching psychic protection from a sliding scale of grey can be invaluable because it reminds you of appropriate responses to any situations you encounter. To illustrate, if you have a cut on your finger, you do not amputate the whole thing! Instead, you use smaller and more appropriate responses to the situation. Instead of amputation, you cleanse and bandage the wound, saving the finger in the process.

While this may seem unrelated to psychic protection, it is actually a very valuable lesson. Proportion should be kept in mind when it comes to responses. This can keep a tight rein on your personal karma as well. If you overreact to a situation, and are aware it is over the top, you have incurred negative karma to deal with as a backlash further on down the road. Yes, you can incur karma by responding to situations in over the top ways. While it does matter whether or not you know your reaction is over the top, it is important to ask yourself if your response is appropriate to the situation. This ties back into issues we discussed earlier, so I'm sure we need not revisit that conversation here.

In Conclusion

Suffice to say, there is a lot more that could be said about the mental plane than what is covered here, but I will not be presumptuous enough to try and address everything related to hypnosis, affirmations, NLP, and other related topics. I would rather leave that to the experts, and while I am putting the work back on your shoulders, it will be more fulfilling if you do the work yourself. After all, what works for you may not necessarily work for me, and vice versa. For example, while I am familiar with affirmations, I have not used them in this way for a great many years. It is a technique I have had great success with in the past, but I have put it aside to refine other techniques more in line with my spiritual path. I do still work with affirmations, but generally from a spiritual perspective rather than a mental one. That approach will be discussed later in the book, but it is worth mentioning here because it shows that a technique or approach you use on one plane can also be used from the perspective of other planes. This liberates us from thinking they are mutually exclusive, or specifically tied to the plane in which they are the most effective or even how they've been introduced in this text.

When confronted with psychic attacks of any kind, it is always wise to take a step back mentally before you react emotionally. It's always best to take a deep breath, and this opens the door to another subject that may seem unrelated, yet can be very powerful; the science of breath.

In Hinduism, there is a branch of Yoga dedicated to breathing, called *pranayama*. I have known about this for years, but it has only been in the last few years that I've made a more determined attempt to put it into practice. Since I have done that, I have noticed that overall I am more composed and in control of my responses to situations. Coupled with developing the skill of having a poker face, it has led my consciousness and personal development in very interesting directions. An intriguing side effect of this development is that it has led to some powerful and interesting gnosis. However, it has also caused my consciousness to develop in ways that are separate and generally alien to the minds of others. Everything comes with a price, though, which is another powerful lesson.

As you develop your proficiency with mental plane subjects and techniques in the name of psychic protection, you will experience unknown or unintended side effects. This is normal and to be expected. While I share some of my experiences above, your experiences will vary, and you will discover different pieces of gnosis on your own that is in line with your spiritual and personal development. The main thing to keep in mind when you notice these side effects is to make sure that they are happening for your greatest growth and good. As much as a mind can be trained in these arts, it can also become unhinged in the process. After all, it is the mind we are discussing here, and by and large where the mind leads, the body follows.

If you are already dealing with psychological conditions and diagnoses, then please consult your mental health care professional before proceeding. As is also true in occultism, working with these forces can unleash powerful forces on the mind, and more than one budding occultist has suffered mentally due to their occult interest and activities. In a perverse inverse of why people turn to psychological related concepts (usually to heal themselves, even though they may not be aware of it at the time), some people who venture into occultism and the paranormal often discover psychological issues that they never knew existed. Unfortunately, many times, this occurs in a very sad and dramatic way. This reinforces the necessity for a structured exploration into whatever part of the subject interests you and requires regular vigilance on your mental state to monitor your psychological stability and progress.

If you find at any time that working with the mental plane is taking a serious, negative toll on your mental health, then focus on the other planes to balance this out. There is such a thing as "too much of a good thing," and the overdevelopment and over-reliance on one plane to the detriment of another can produce sickness and worse. A good everyday application of this is that when your

Psychic Protection

emotions get too strong to control, you pour that energy into a different project, such as a physical exercise routine, or in my case, cleaning the house. This burns out the adrenaline and exhausts me physically, creating emotional detachment. I am quite frankly too tired to engage in the emotions, so am able to view the situation more clearly, not influenced by emotions. Always observe the whole of your life, not just one particular area of it, for we do not know where and when we will need to protect ourselves, and the best form of defense is often a good offense.

Chapter Eight
Critical Thinking Tips

We're now going to turn our attention to various thoughts and tips that I put under the blanket of critical thinking. There are many other critical thinking techniques out there that I will not include here, largely because I don't know them. I say this because the subject of critical thinking skills has long been studied regarding philosophy and related subjects, and I defer to their centuries-old wisdom. Logical and critical thinking skills are easily found for those who desire to know more. And, bluntly, I never really got into philosophy. It always seemed too passive to me, and the wisdom of the East was more vibrant and applicable to my young mind when I first learned of these subjects. That bias I developed decades ago still exists within me to this day, and I have no intention of changing it, for reasons that are not only outside the scope of this book but are also personal.

However, what we will discuss here are critical thinking examples of metaphysical wisdom I have picked up over the years that I have found very helpful when it comes to protecting the mind against those who might try to dull my senses and cause me to lose my light. In this way, the concepts here are somewhat hodge-podge within the chapter, but they are all related in that they can be of great value and assistance regarding mental protection. If you know of other techniques and insights in addition to what is discussed here, then add all of this to your repertoire. Remember that the more you increase your palette; the more spirit can bring you, because you can receive more.

As we move forward, we must first reinforce the knowledge of one of the core concepts of magick. This is that we are constantly creating, or co-creating, our reality in line with our Will, every minute of every day. This also serves to remind us how powerful we truly are, but with that comes increased responsibilities. It is easy to lose track of this if one is the subject of a psychic attack of any nature, which is why reminders are always good. This philosophy should be tempered with other concepts such as humility, genetic karma, and other limiting factors discussed previously, but overall it is a good philosophy to work with and evolve.

The Now

Through the last twenty years, this topic has received widespread acclaim and criticism, with both occurring for good reason. The concept of "the now" is quite simple. We live in an eternal moment, with no past and no future. This has been adopted from particular Eastern traditions, especially Buddhism, and has been brought into the Western world through the technological evolution that has begun to interconnect the planet. I have known many people over the years who work religiously with this concept in a very healthy fashion, but I have also known many who work with it in a toxic way, based on denial , so be careful if you are interacting with people who claim to work with this on a regular basis.

The core concept is a good one. It tells us to be mindful of our thoughts. If we worry about things or are always living in or reflecting on the past, our attention is not on the present, which is where the power is. After all, our memories of the past are over and done with. We may still have strong emotional attachments to them, but they are gone. I realize this sounds cold, but that is simply a fact. What causes pain in situations like this is our emotional attachment to whatever those memories are. Some people will say that the lesson here is to detach and focus on the moment. While I largely agree with that, there is still the fact that the very people telling you that may be living in denial of things from their past. The part of this I do not agree with is simply shifting your consciousness to the present, because it could lead to denial or psychosis. Rather, before you embark on this teaching, do yourself one big favor first: Heal.

We often reflect on the past because of some sort of emotional trauma, or sometimes emotional victory, so it can take some serious work to move forward. Setting this unhealed wound aside is one of the most damaging things you can do to yourself. Enacting healing in order to move forward may be what is needed before embracing the concept of living in the eternal moment. It is quite healthy, natural, and normal, to still reflect on emotional situations of the past, but you should be careful not to get stuck there. Even if this is a gradual progression, as long as it continues, spiritual and personal growth will occur, and that can be more valuable than living in the now.

From a more severe perspective, this kind of thinking and behavior can lead to psychoses of various kinds. If you simply stop thinking about the past, then it becomes harder to be aware of the consequences of your actions, and eventually it becomes impossible to accept the consequences of actions at all. If this disregard is present, it can easily spiral out of control into unhealthy behavior patterns. To me, it is quite psychotic to be so focused on the moment that you lose sight of cause and effect, action and reaction, and action and consequences. This can lead to a total disrespect and abuse of others around you. I have known a few people like that in the past, but they are in the minority. This cautionary tale serves as a stark reminder to be eternally vigilant.

Since Lewis Carroll is right, ("It's a poor sort of memory

that only works backwards." – from *Alice in Wonderland*), we should now turn our attention to the converse. What if we were to spend all of our time and energy focusing on the future? The end result would be the same in that our attention and therefore our power would not be in the moment, so we would be denying ourselves personal power and potential impact on those around us. The difference, though, is that most people are not thinking of an emotional trauma when they are thinking about the future. Most people are daydreaming, lost in fantasyland, and usually this is motivated by escapism, turning their attention away from their current life situation. The moral issues and dilemmas from the past don't necessarily compare with this, but what we get instead is simply someone who is not paying attention to what is occurring around them. In this way they are still choosing to deny themselves their own personal power over the moment, but through careless behavior and half-thought through decisions. While reflecting backwards does indicate strong emotional and empathic affinity, looking forwards indicates someone who is highly creative with many ideas. Too many, almost, because they have more than they can bring down into physical manifestation. Developing the element of earth is good for these people because it draws their attention back to the present, and it physically produces results.

It is wise to focus on the present whenever we can, but we should be careful to protect ourselves from the pitfalls discussed above. It is through our unhealed wounds and lazy minds that we can be attacked, or at least be manipulated into thinking we are being attacked when it is our own demons getting to us. As with all things, temper this teaching and approach with common sense and an application especially in line with your spiritual path.

One of the ways to make sure you are staying on top of this is through the use of affirmations and periodic internal reflection and review. When do you pause to reflect on what has happened before? This is harder to do if you don't keep a journal, but if you do, you already have the best starting material you could ask for. Just make sure that you keep it up to date. I have found that the best review cycle is one that lines up with a particular rhythm in your life. For example, I usually do it around the first day of each season, but some people do it once a year, perhaps on their birthday or at the festival of the New Year. It is really up to you when and how frequently you want to do this review but building it into your routine life is good to do, simply so you can track your growth. The basic concept here is simply that if your life is improving, then your spiritual and personal growth is successful. If things are falling apart, you may want to re-evaluate what you're doing, and why. The caveat that comes up here, though, is that sometimes circumstances have to disintegrate before they can get better, so sometimes your life will dip down before rising to new heights of greatness. Since your analysis of this is subjective and unique to you, you have to use your best judgment when applying it to what you're going through, so there isn't much I can say on the matter from an objective perspective. Just be aware that this is a possibility, and if that is the case, then remember that every night has its dawn.

Focus and Discipline

A person cannot serve two masters. This is one of the most important things to keep in mind when it comes to personal and spiritual development. Where is your focus? Is it on the spiritual and the uplifting, or is it on lower ego gratification? It is not my place to pass any kind of judgment on another's choices concerning their spiritual path, but I simply point this out for you to notice and contemplate. The true essence of this teaching is to ask yourself where your focus is, and of course in a perfect world it should always be on the spiritual and developmental perspective, but hey, we're all humans. Your attention is going to waver from time to time, and there is nothing wrong with this. The key is to simply keep working on improving your discipline and focus as you go through life. Being aware of your strengths and growth opportunities puts you in a better position to self-evaluate, and reflection is always a good thing.

Practicing thought control, especially control of your own thoughts, is what is achieved by addressing both of these points. Many people think thought control applies only when it comes to the thoughts of others, but that is only one side of the equation. The other side is that you can apply this same idea to policing your own thoughts. This is one of the best mental plane defense tools I have discovered. By being in firm control of your thoughts, you protect yourself from the ability of other people to influence you in ways that could be detrimental. All this takes is discipline, and can be easier said than done, but it is still true none the less. The cultivation of mental focus and discipline can bleed over into other areas of your life, producing surprising results, and this reinforces the call for vigilance. Some of the best psychic protection you can have is the ability to remain calm, cool, and detached when everyone else has succumbed to the emotions of the situation. While I prefer the tools of the mental plane, (in essence what we have been discussing in these last two chapters), we should note another pitfall related to it, which is dogma.

Dogma

According to the Oxford Dictionary, dogma is defined as "a belief or set of beliefs held by a group or organization, which others are expected to accept without argument." In other words, it refers to being in a group and its beliefs cannot be argued with or critically examined - basically, if you have ever been in a group and you are not allowed to question anything, and other members are very offended if you do. This may even extend to the point of ostracism and/or emotional repercussions within the community. This can be a tricky topic, and again is highly subjective to various factors, but in toxic groups dogma can be a powerful tool of control, usually by sick people. In a healthy spiritual system, dogma would be very light. Why is this, you ask?

Everything in reality needs a structure of some kind in order to grow. Everything needs boundaries and limits. After all, "growth for growth's sake is the ideology of a cancer cell." (Edward Abbey). So in this regard, dogma is good because it helps create structure and set limits. However, problems arise when there is too much dogma, or it is used in a malicious way as discussed above. Yes, develop your mental plane tools. Yes, cultivate your own spiritual system. But, be careful not to get so stuck on or in it that you don't allow room for spontaneous growth. This idea has been passed down over the centuries in the form of the esoteric teaching that if you think you know everything, you generally don't know anything. The wise person is confident in their knowledge, yes, but should not be so ego driven that they are completely set in their ways, so they cannot learn anything new or change what they do know into a higher state of being. Astrologically speaking, this is a lesson of Saturn. Structure builds foundation.

Why is it so necessary to be aware of dogma? From a social perspective, guarding against this can keep you out of harm's way when it comes to cults. Secondly, people may try to manipulate you through the application of dogma via the method of guilt. Finally, and this is an important one, if someone says that what they know is the be-all-end-all, this is a red flag to think twice about them and their teachings. No one person, myself included, has a corner on teachings of any kinds. Sure, some people may be right about a lot of things, but they are humble enough to recognize their limits, and are open minded enough to listen to alternative points of view. After all, if a belief cannot stand up to scrutiny, how strong is the belief, really? A true belief can be challenged and still hold up, at least if it is any good. How do you know when to question things you hear, other than the previously mentioned discussion on dogma? The answer to that is the segue to the next section of this chapter. Consider the source in all things.

Consider the Source…

…in all things. A serious point to note, this is a very powerful but also a very touchy subject. When you hear or read new information, consider its source. What does the informer have to gain by telling you the information? More importantly, do they know what they're talking about? For example, when I learn more information to improve my business skills, I research people who are successful businesspeople, and haven't declared bankruptcy. When I want to improve my cooking skills, I learn from people who can cook, not someone who can't.

You can see how this could become touchy very quickly. After all, what if the businessman had to declare bankruptcy because the laws changed? Well, on one hand, they still became bankrupt, so their foresight and certain aspects of what they have to teach could still wrong and ultimately doomed to fail. But, on the other hand, you can't fault them for making that decision if they simply found themselves in a bad situation. This line of thinking can also be extended into who you learn from. Do you pay attention to people who have demonstrated competence, or do you learn from people who have only read about something and have no experience under their belt? There is a correct answer to this, which is that you should learn from someone who is proficient in the skill you're researching, rather than someone who has only read about it. Yes, there should be a good balance of theory and practice, but at the end of the day you need both to be successful. When in doubt, remember that "an ounce of action is worth a ton of theory." (Ralph Waldo Emerson). Again, be careful with this, because if you rely on it too much, you might miss buried wisdom from unexpected places. I'm sure the esoteric application is clear here, so I won't dwell on it too much, but it is worth keeping in mind, because it helps prevent being conned by people who don't know about a subject yet are trying to make you belief they do; generally for nefarious purposes. This can best be summed up by a quote from the late Dr Timothy Leary: "To think for yourself, you must question authority..." Or, as Donald Michael Kraig has said, "Think for yourself, question everything." Yes, question the source of all things, and this includes yourself. For example, as of this writing I have never been married, so when people ask me for romantic insight or advice, I am generally very careful to keep things focused on healthy communication, compassion, and other foundational pieces of healthy relationships, and that's about it. I keep in mind that my knowledge may be limited, and I should be careful not to speak out of my element. You wouldn't learn rocketry from a banker, so why would you not use this same line of thinking when it comes to your spiritual and personal growth?

Asking the Right Questions

This may seem obvious but does merit inclusion as a mental plane tool of protection. It can be summarized into one main question to ask yourself when you are confronted with major decisions in life: "Is this for my greatest growth and good?" In her important book, "Ask the Right

Questions," Debbie Ford actually provides ten questions to flesh this out, but here we'll focus upon this fundamental question. Sometimes psychic attackers will try to dull our senses so that we make poor and even damaging decisions, so by keeping this is mind, we make it harder for them to influence us in negative ways.

In addition to asking this about yourself, extend it out to include your loved ones. How will the decision you are about to make going to affect them? If you are in a position of leadership, how will this decision impact them? By doing this, you also create an opportunity to stop, center, focus, and ground, so that you can see the situation clearly with less influence from others. This technique also keeps you focused on self-development and aimed at making the best life you can for yourself and your loved ones.

Predatory Consciousness

The title of this section may sound scary, and that is intentional on my part, because I want to stress how powerful and intimidating this concept can be, but also how misunderstood it usually is. The consciousness of a predator has certain characteristics that can be helpful when exercising psychic protection. After all, which would you rather be in life, predator or prey? Part of this concerns living life with confidence, and another part concerns thinking in proactive ways. After all, the best way to deal with potential psychic attacks is to do your best to make sure you don't find yourself in that situation in the first place! As trite as it sounds, it is true. This isn't a one hundred percent set-in-stone rule, though, and there are exceptions to it. Sometimes you can do your best and still be involved in a sticky situation, so while this is a good goal to strive for, it is still not an absolute destination. Thus, avoidance is not something to work towards, but it is good to be aware of, regardless.

Another earmark of predatory consciousness is that of being proactive rather than reactive, and really that is the whole focus of this book. This, and every other book on psychic protection out there, are written with the intent of helping you be proactive so that your energy remains safe and protected. In this way the books are predatory in nature, and some of them even in tone. See? Predatory consciousness isn't so bad. It's a lot like the concept of manipulation. Generally, people believe manipulation is a dirty word, but if we were in a room together and I asked you to close the door, then technically I am manipulating you, but in this case, it is something harmless and theoretically, potentially something good. So to say that manipulation is always bad is to misunderstand what it is, and how intent can influence situations that are neutral and make them either good or bad, depending on the whim of the person doing the manipulating. This is also true of predatory consciousness. It is a state of being, in which you are aware of your own personal power and can use it effectively in many areas of life in order to achieve success. Problems only arise if you allow base desires and gratification to get in the way of true evolution and maturity.

Another characteristic of this kind of consciousness is that you can also make a habit of creating win-win situations periodically throughout life. This kind of situation takes skill to develop, but when you do cultivate it, you can achieve more success than if you don't. To develop it, though, takes a shift in consciousness more than anything else. The shift is that in order to create win-win situations, you must first develop the ability to see all situations in life as possible win-wins. Some people, especially those who are pessimists, may be challenged by this, and to be blunt, it took me a while to learn it myself, so if you struggle with developing this ability, I can sympathize. I've been in your shoes, and all I can say is that one of the best things you can do is to reflect on various

Psychic Protection

situations in your life. See what benefits you got out of situations that you thought were "losses." This is related to the idea that you should be careful, because you might get what you thought you wanted, and it might not be what you really want at all, or maybe more than you bargained for. After you can see the majority of situations in your life from a win-win situation, you are then in a position to train yourself to create them for yourself, in line with your Will.

Interestingly enough, this is a fantastic psychic protection technique to develop, because it makes it harder for psychic attackers to throw you off your center. If you train yourself to see the positive in all situations, or at least the 'win,' then those that would normally negatively impact you emotionally no longer do so. You will be more prepared for the unexpected. This can also have side effects that expedite your spiritual growth because ultimately it brings your attention full circle to the power and necessity of the moment mentioned at the start this chapter. This is one of the ways you can intertwine the two. By adapting a proactive consciousness, you become in control of what truly matters – your reaction to everything that comes your way.

As for many things in life, the power is in the response, and the person who cares the least usually controls the situation the most. I don't think I need to discuss the many, many exceptions to this that you may be thinking of, but they do exist. By and large, though, this is a good way to live. Not only does it frustrate psychic attackers, it also helps to further discipline your mind in a proactive and healthy way. When you realize this, you also realize that how you prioritize things is of major importance when it comes to protecting yourself. A teaching I learned many years ago is to not sweat the small stuff, and it's all small stuff. The motivational speaker Stuart Wilde spoke of this, and eventually, after many experiences spread out over many years, it finally sunk in, and became one of the more valuable teachings I have used in the name of psychically protecting myself. Often, no reaction is the clearest reaction of all, and not all events in life require a response. Before you respond, you should ask yourself if you should, and if you decide to, then you should do your best to react from a space of clear, mental thought.

What the ideas in this chapter call for is discernment. By choosing what to focus on and where to spend our attention and energy, we insulate ourselves against those who might try to attack us energetically. Remembering how to prioritize, and improving our ability to do so, can be invaluable and can train our consciousness in the process. This allows for more spiritual gnosis and personal success to come through in day to day life. Knowing when to address a situation versus when not to can save a lot of headaches and emotional heartbreak. Knowing how to respond seals the deal for mentally protecting yourself. With these two points in mind, you can handle almost anything that comes your way. Of course, you can also see how powerful this can be when used in conjunction with other techniques discussed in this section, and it is always good to experiment with different combinations to see what works best for you. These are not mutually exclusive and should be combined to produce powerful effects in your life. When you turn your attention to being proactive with these techniques, instead of only using them to react to situations, you open up a whole new dimension of experiences that can further your personal growth, hasten your spiritual ascent, and improve the quality of your life in general. And really, all of this is only the beginning of the development of your mind. The material we are discussing here can be used as preliminary work for what you read in *Spirit Relations*, or it can be used as stand-alone material for your own psychic protection. Regardless, remember that in this case it is truly the intent that determines how things play out.

Occam's Razor

Finally, I want to close this chapter discussing one of my favorite principles from philosophy, that of Occam's Razor. Named for its progenitor William of Ockham, it basically suggests that if you are faced with a situation that has two possible explanations, the simplest is usually the correct one. I really like this idea because it can be applied to many, many things, and a lot of them protective in orientation. A good example of this is the craving for a hamburger. You may look at this metaphysically and think that your body needs the meat to ground, and yes, that might be true from a metaphysical perspective. Or, it could simply be that you want a hamburger, nothing deeper than that.

To summarize, the fewer deductions, suppositions, and speculations, the more accurate the answer probably is. This reminds me a lot of how energy follows the path of least resistance through the multiverse, and thus I find a resonance with it. It reminds us life is all about simplicity. The human mind does have a tendency to see things that are not there, or to blow things out of proportion, both of which enforce the necessity for mental discipline in the name of safety. Occam's Razor can be very useful to keep us grounded in the here and now, and not read too far into things. Yes, there is generally a metaphysical cause for how things manifest in the physical world, but we should never rule out what is directly in front of us. However, we should also not ignore the metaphysical in the name of the physical. After all, everything is intertwined.

As we draw to a close, we can turn our attention to the next plane, the spiritual plane. While at the higher end of the mental plane ideas shift from hard logic and reason to abstract thought, it is also true that we move into a blending place for the spiritual plane. The highest part of the mental plane is the lowest part of the spiritual plane, so for the final section of this book, we will look at more spiritually themed techniques and tools. Remember, though, that there are many more spiritual techniques, practices, and tools, than I can list here. Rather, I will present key points and highlights that work for me. If you have specialized media that addresses your spiritual path directly, now would be the time to pull that information out and have it at the ready, for some of the things we will talk about have counterparts in many different pantheons that I may not mention here.

And, now that we have come this far, take a moment to reflect on the essence of psychic protection. The essence is your approach to life. How do you project yourself? Are you self-confident? Are you disciplined and focused upon ways that can improve your life? If your answer to these questions are positive, then you are probably already protecting yourself more than you realize. If you could use some work in those areas, then turn your attention to those first and foremost, but as you do, be aware that you will be causing ripples and changes in your daily life, so be prepared and proactive, and you will achieve success.

Section Four
Spiritual Tools

Chapter Nine
Daily Spiritual Regimen

Continuing the theme that alignment with your spiritual path is of primary importance, I would like to open this chapter with a simple point: that your daily spiritual regiment is completely in line with your spiritual beliefs – but I emphasize this: As long as you have a daily spiritual regiment!

Having such a routine is a wise and practical practice to establish. It can lead to enhanced spiritual and personal growth and adds a layer of protection against those who would do you harm. It accomplishes three important things. First, it keeps your personal energy clear. Second, it keeps your mind spiritually focused. Third, the energetic strength generated through the repeated pattern can act as an energetic bubble of protection that immediately makes it harder for energetic beings to attach themselves. I have found all three are of major importance when it comes to self-protection and advancing your spiritual growth. Yet at the same time, it requires the much-loathed skill of self-discipline, which is why many people do not engage in it. But the rewards are worth the effort, at least as my experience has taught me. I have been performing a daily spiritual regiment for almost twenty years, and have found it of immense value and assistance, so I do encourage its exploration at least.

The practice consists of activities focused on your spiritual and personal development, but beyond that it's a concept that is largely subjective and includes activities from your belief system. Since I have never walked a mile in your shoes, there's not much I can say beyond that. However, what we will be discussing are examples from various traditions to spur your imagination, and also to show you some of the techniques available, that can be used in conjunction with more pantheon-specific techniques. Some of these are generic thoughts you can apply to many spiritual paths, and you can adapt these easily to what you believe and how you practice it. This makes them more like the execution of principles in a sense.

Pantheons

The first and most important suggestion to note is to *know your pantheon*! Almost every pantheon has at least one protective deity, and through personal workings you can contact them and develop a relationship with them for your own protection. A pantheon is a collection of spiritual beings (usually referred to as gods and/or goddesses) that are generally tied to a particular society or culture. They often have similar traits and strong connections to each other and an overall theme that binds them together. For example, a lot, if not most of the Hindu pantheon have correspondences concerned with consciousness and the manipulation thereof. This serves as a strong reminder to learn about who you are working with spiritually, and to discover as much about them as possible in order to make a stronger, deeper connection. This can be a lifelong process, and the journey itself an exercise in growth. The gods are a part of us, and because of this, when we work with them, we are activating parts of ourselves.

Everyone has a preferred pantheon to work with, even if it is one of their own making. Everyone works with multiple deities, even if there is a hierarchy within their chosen system. For example, someone can be a Christian, meaning they predominantly work with God, but rest assured that they also work with Jesus, Mary, or saints and angels. This may be to a lesser extent, but it is generally true. It is relatively uncommon for people to work only with one deity, but it does happen.

Take a few moments to think or write down who or what comprises your pantheon. These may include beings deriving from the same culture, such as if someone works with the Celtic pantheon, but these beings do not necessarily have to share the same cultural background. This often occurs when someone creates their own pantheon. There is nothing wrong with this, and by and large people do it all the time. However, a lot of people work with the pantheon of one particular culture, excluding all others. Some people even work with multiple pantheons, but there is usually a preference of one over the other. Sometimes, this may involve two different pantheons, such as in the case of someone who works with the Celtic and Norse systems. Other times this can be an existing pantheon in conjunction with a pantheon of one's personal creation. Really it doesn't matter, and it is up to you how you choose to do it. It is stronger to work with pantheons that already exist, but that does not mean those are the only ones available to you.

And, while we're on the subject, let's talk about the gods and goddesses for more insight and to stimulate the imagination. Let's apply a little bit of pragmatism to this much vaunted concept. I always like to discuss this point because we live at a very interesting time in the evolution of our species, and a lot of people are trying new and different things in a spiritual sense. I know many people who are experimenting with unconventional pantheons, and while from the outside this might appear crazy or silly to practitioners who prefer a more conventional approach, the experimenters are living out behavior that has been passed down through the centuries.

What I'm talking about here are people who work with

pantheons that derive from popular culture. I know many people who have begun working with characters that originated in video games, movies, novels and stories and even TV series. While, to some, this might seem delusional, but when we take a closer look at it, we find some very interesting magical principles at work. First, if you really stop and think about it, this must be the way that most pantheons were created back in the early years of their formation. Someone has an idea. They share it with others, and over time, all of this energy coalesces into the beings that correspond to the stories they are sharing. Recent discoveries and evidence tells us that statues from the Greco-Roman period were painted in much the same way people paint statues now, in very dynamic colors and color schemes. This reminds me a lot of how people paint models today.

This means that when someone begins to work with an unconventional pantheon, they are walking in the same footsteps as millions of people throughout the centuries before them. While you might find it uncomfortable to accept people working with the pantheon from the Star Wars universe, or even from Pokémon, these systems are as valid as others that have been around for centuries longer. There are far fewer people working with either one of those pantheons as there were with older deities, but this doesn't necessarily mean they are less effective. Some people say that this approach falls under the category of pop culture magick or chaos magick, and as far as its categorization here goes, I share no opinion, because it is really none of my business, and if it works for them, then so be it. Simply know that this illustrates how liberally you can view and interact with a pantheon, so let your imagination be your guide.

Common and popular pantheons include: Celtic, Norse, Hindu, Egyptian, Sumerian, Hebrew, Christian, Native American, Zoroastrianism, Greek, Roman, and many,

many others, depending on where you live and various other factors. The best way to begin working with a pantheon, if you haven't already, is to study the history of your own culture. This can either be the society you live or were raised in, or the culture that is found through various DNA tests and other means, such as family history. Another way to find a pantheon that works for you is to listen to your intuition and see if you feel a strong energetic connection with a particular one, because there is probably some reason why it calls to you. This can be based on soul memories or comfort, or some other reason unbeknownst to you or me. Folklore tales can also be a profound source of insight as well and should not be neglected in your research.

Some people claim that you will have the strongest connection with a pantheon deriving from your homeland or home soil. For example, I currently live in the USA, and therefore, following this line of logic through, I would have a natural affinity for the belief systems and pantheons indigenous to North America, which would include Satanism, Native American spiritual beliefs, Mormonism, and Scientology. What a diverse selection! Personally though, I have found a strong connection with native teachings, specifically Native American ones, but as to the rest on the list? I don't really feel a connection with them at all. I mention this here because it can be a good starting point if you are unfamiliar with this concept.

Protection Deities

Almost all, if not all, of these pantheons have protective deities that can be called upon during times of stress and duress. This point is worth keeping in mind because it brings up a very valuable insight: If you have to call constantly upon protection deities, then you may want to reevaluate what you are doing spiritually. After all, if you are constantly being attacked or feeling like you are being attacked, then there is something seriously wrong with your spiritual and personal growth, or at least the system you are using.

Most protection deities generally appear as very scary or intimidating when you search for images of them, and of course this is intentional. The stories as to why they are this way is generally connected with the spiritual and cultural context that led to their creation, which reinforces the reasons why research is so important. Their fierce visages are meant to intimidate the beings they square off against, but also to intimidate those who want to work with them. After all, if you're not strong enough to face these fierce looking deities, then do you really have the strength to face malevolent forces in general?

Not all protection deities are the same, which is important to keep in mind when you are working with them. The specific point I am addressing here is that not all protection deities are violent, or strengthening, or possess any other particular characteristics. Be careful when you reach out to them now that you know this, because you may get more than you bargained for when you start this relationship. Here is a hypothetical situation to illustrate the point. If you are generally a pacifist, and you find yourself in a position where you want to work with a protection deity from your pantheon, you might be quite put off if your life takes a more intense and possibly violence-filled turn after you start the relationship. Yet that is what you really asked for – protection. You just didn't specify how you wanted it, or maybe you picked the wrong deity with whom to engage. Continuing our conversation from the previous two chapters, one of the ways to avoid problems like this is to expand your consciousness to see your situation in a new light from a different perspective. This could lead you to work with familiar deities from the pantheon in new and different ways. As you can see, this can increase your spiritual and personal growth faster than you might have anticipated.

Law of Vibration and Resonance

One of the best things you can do to work with protective deities from your chosen pantheon is to make sure you feel comfortable when in their presence and with having them in your life. You will achieve a stronger connection with them if you do. Sometimes this comfort can be established in your physical space, through creating altars and shrines, but in can also be accomplished by making your mind, heart, and spirit conducive to the deities' residence. For example, if you are working with a protection deity that is known for its aggression, then it would be wise to carry yourself with confidence and engage in proactivity. If you want to work with protective beings, then you should cultivate your personal strength. If you are working with a more aggressive protective being, then being more aggressive in your day to day life would be wise to do. I don't think I need to give any more examples to illustrate the point, as I'm sure it is clear that you want to establish a resonance with the being so it may align with you. It is through this alignment that you can cultivate a deeper and stronger relationship more conducive to success than if you just prayed to them and didn't make them feel welcome. A more important spiritual lesson here is that you want to make the being comfortable in your company, just as you would when conversing with a person. The more you remember to use the same principles you would use when dealing with human beings, the more success you will have when dealing with nonphysical beings.

Solar Alignment

While technically an optional protection technique, this

can still be an excellent way to align yourself spiritually and to send safer, stronger energy into the universe to dissuade would-be energetic attackers. In short, this is a broad category and usually includes solar worshipping. However, this can also be extended to include religious and spiritual traditions that include specific times to pray. While I list these two as examples here, I'm sure that with a little creative thinking you can find other ways to break up the day and set aside time to align yourself with a being greater than yourself. I'll break down two commonly encountered daily regimen to illustrate my point. If you know more, then you will have a greater sample to draw from while we continue this discussion. You can also be pioneering and develop your own daily spiritual practice. For example, I work a lot with the Egyptian god Anpu (Anubis), and he had two specific times of day sacred to him: dawn and dusk. At both of these times the veil between the worlds is believed to be thinnest, a time when it is easy to have a foot in both worlds, the physical and the nonphysical. This generally isn't mentioned a lot in current conversations on the topic, but it illustrates how you can think outside the box if you decide to create your own timetable for spiritual practices.

Solar Adorations

This is the most common form of daily adoration, and as you can tell by the name, it is based on the cycle of the sun over the course of a day. The most common structured form of this practice you will encounter dates back thousands of years but has been changed and modified throughout the centuries. However, its essence remains the same. This also means it is a good framework if you want to adapt it to your own beliefs. There are four times of the day that this procedure is usually performed: sunrise (or when you wake up), noon (or when the sun is at its height),

Psychic Protection

twilight, and finally midnight (or when you go to sleep).

Because of the source of the oldest recorded solar adoration, the deities called on of Ancient Egyptian origin, but you will see when looking at the structure that you could easily replace the Egyptian deities with whatever alternatives make you feel comfortable. I will list the most common form of this below, and you will notice it is very formulaic. This makes it easier to construct if you choose to create your own version, and it also makes it easier to memorize. Anyway, enough with the ambiguities. Let's lay it out for digestion:

At dawn (or when you wake up), face east (The direction of the rising Sun):

Hail unto thee, who art Ra in thy rising,
Even unto thee who art Ra in thy strength,
Who travellest over the heavens in thy bark at the uprising of the Sun.
Tehuti standeth at his splendor at the prow and Ra-Hoor abideth at the helm!
Hail unto thee from the abodes of night!

At noon, face south, the direction of the sun at its height. (Keep in mind though, this is only correct if you are in the northern hemisphere of the planet. If you are in the southern hemisphere, you would face north):

Hail unto thee who art Hathor in thy triumphing,
Even unto thee who art Hathor in thy beauty,
Who travellest over the heavens in thy bark at the mid-course of the Sun!
Tehuti standeth at his splendor at the prow and Ra-Hoor abideth at the helm!
Hail unto thee from the abodes of morning!

At twilight, face west. (The direction of the setting sun):

Bill Duvendack

Hail unto thee who art Tum in thy setting,
Even unto thee who art Tum in thy joy,
Who travellest over the heavens in thy bark at the down going of the Sun!
Tehuti standeth in his splendor at the prow and Ra-Hoor abideth at the helm!
Hail unto thee from the abodes of day!

Finally, at midnight, or before you go to bed, face north (If you are in the southern hemisphere, you would face South):

Hail unto thee who art Khepra in thy hiding,
Even unto thee who art Khepra in thy silence,
Who travellest over thy heavens in thy bark at the midnight hour of the Sun!
Tehuti standeth at his splendor at the prow and Ra-Hoor abideth at the helm!
Hail unto thee from the abodes of the evening!

The particular phrasing used above is from the writings of Aleister Crowley, and while it is in line with the original material, it does vary slightly. It is found in *Liber Resh vel Helios*, which is easy to track down for those of you who like it. As we take a closer look at it, we can see that it is written in stanza form and is very much a template. I like to point this out because it suggests that if you use the template, it is easy to adjust to your personal preferences. Now it also becomes clear (as I mentioned earlier) about the incorporation of Egyptian gods. You can swap them out for other deities you may prefer, but keep in mind that they should align with the particular times of the day during which they are called. In addition to the words and directions mentioned above, there are also various body postures Mr. Crowley included in his writings, but these are not mandatory. I have found the body gestures help to align with these energies, but you might feel differently.

Or, you may find other body postures in line with your spiritual path that would be more appropriate. This may take a lot of research on your part and even experimentation, but in the end it is worth it. I can tell you that from personal experience.

Performing a sun adoration has an interesting powerful side effect that you would be wise to note. Often, by repeating this for an extended period of time, you will align yourself with the cycles of the Sun. I'm not joking or exaggerating when I say that. I have experienced this, as have many others I have spoken with over the years, and the precision of this never ceases to impress me. Many times, I have turned my attention to the clock only to see it is the exact time for the next solar adoration in the sequence. This is a very real and physical alignment that is occurring, which can be of great value for those who like to maximize what they can accomplish in a day in order to practice living a life of abundance. This technique also keeps our attention on the moment and can increase our awareness and discipline for accomplishing what we desire.

Another example of a daily adoration is found in the religion of Islam. In short, there are five times a day that a good Muslim will turn his attention to the direction of their holy city of Mecca. This is known as *Salah*. They then lay out their prayer blanket, drop to their knees, and pray to Allah. If they are unable to fall to their knees for various health reasons, they can skip this requirement, as long as they still execute their prayer. There are many more components to this practice than I mention here, but since this makes it more complex than solar adorations, I leave the details out in the name of brevity. This practice serves as a good example of how you can approach a daily spiritual regiment without focusing it on the sun. Some of the Muslim times are solar focused, but other times they are not. If you are considering making your own daily adorations, you may want to consider researching this further to see the various variations to stimulate your imagination for creating your own.

Technically, you don't have to align yourself with the sun, but it is simply the easiest focus to use. If you think of all of this as a ritual, then also consider the fact that everyone has rituals they execute throughout the day at particular times, so it should be easy to convert your consciousness to include more spiritual foci. While you may find it better to use an adoration that already exists, it is always powerful and fun to create your own when you are ready, as you see fit.

Symbolism

Another trait common to many spiritual systems is that of symbolism. Symbolism is one of the most powerful subjects you can ever study or use, so I suggest you enjoy studying it. As a matter of fact, for a lot of the twentieth century, psychological professionals have studied the effects of symbols on the subconscious, and in recent decades this has expanded to include hypnotists and practitioners of other related fields.

So, what are symbols? First, they are not words. This means that when we work with them, they bypass the conscious mind and go straight to the subconscious. This also means they are retained more strongly and last longer in the mind than the many words we encounter over the course of the day.

As the concept applies to our work here, there are protective symbols which are unique to different spiritual systems that are protective in nature, and when applicable, they should be sought out and used. For example, in Christianity a cross is a commonly worn symbol of faith and protection. In ancient Egyptian beliefs, the Eye of

Horus was known as a protective symbol. Another that has gained popularity in recent years is the Hamsa hand from the Middle East. These are just a few examples from a plethora of spiritual traditions that span the globe, so I'm sure you can easily find symbols that derive from your spiritual path that can aid you in your protective measures.

And hey, if all else fails, why not *make* a protective symbol for your journey? After all, personalizing your path is one of the hallmarks of the true spiritual seeker. I have known people through the years who have kept trinkets that formerly belonged to loved ones, and while they called these their "good luck tokens," really they were protective items that were symbolic, and thus held power and meaning to the bearer. This makes them just as potent as any established symbol in the world today and therefore they should not be underestimated. Just because they're not traditional does not make them impotent.

There is plenty of information available to those who want to learn more, and I strongly encourage you to seek out the information you feel is best appropriate to help your defense for those times you feel you need it. This can also lead to a deeper study on how to make your own holy symbols, which in turn can open the door to sigils and automatic writing and drawing, so symbols truly open a portal to a whole new level of spiritual ascent and attainment.

Mantras

I get kind of twitchy about this subject, because I have a lot of experience with mantras through a dear friend and teacher of mine now in Spirit. I'm not going to name drop but suffice to say it was a quality education. He and his wife taught me a lot about Hinduism, which is the origin of mantras. Mantras are *specific* to the Hindu tradition, and the word itself is Sanskrit. There's simply no discussion past that to be had. However, almost every spiritual system out there has something comparable, and while they are usually similar, they are not mantras! Period. It gets old seeing misguided and disrespectful information out there about mantras. Mantras are Hindu, and yet while they are from that spiritual system, they can be used outside of it quite easily in a modular fashion with other spiritual systems. Essentially, this makes them spiritual technology rather than something belief-fueled and intrinsic to their native system.

The theory of mantras is quite simple, and at this time in history, fairly well-known. Mantras are based on manipulating sound frequencies, thereby affecting vibrations. When we chant something in a particular way, certain energetic patterns come into being, and over extended use they can manipulate reality. In Hinduism, the seed sound of all creation is the "OM," so when mantras are chanted, they are generally based on this baseline.

Breaking down the details, each letter in a mantra is a letter from the Sanskrit alphabet. Like Hebrew, there are a multitude of correspondences associated with each letter, and it is through chanting them that their abilities are accessed. The other half of the equation, or rather how they make the magick, as it were, is that each one of us has an energetic body that parallels the physical form. The most common name for this is the chakra system, again from Hinduism, but it is also known by other titles, such as in Theosophy where it is simply "The Etheric Double." Residing in this energy body are conduits from major concentrations of energy that flow into each other. These pools are known as chakras, and they whirl and swim as they are pooled there. These interdimensional energy vortices are altered and changed when one chants mantras. What this means is that when we are chanting mantras, we are altering the energy as it moves through our bodies, but also changing what we emit into the multiverse around us. So, we are changing our reality by energetically reprogramming ourselves to project differently, more in line with our Will.

There are many mantras for protection available from Hinduism, and with minimal effort, you can find the right mantra for the job in hand. Beyond that, all you need is a little knowledge to get started. I assure you though, this is a very brief and down and dirty introduction to mantras. The best introductory book has already been written in the form of *Healing Mantras* by Thomas Ashley-Farrand. I am going to clarify a lot of things so that if you see wrong or false information out there, you know how to treat it. To undertake a proper basic mantra discipline means you say the same mantra 108 times for 40 days in a row. There are variations on this and note that this is the *basic* information you need to know to get started.

Some people will tell you that you need a mala, (a string of prayer beads) and while I do think this is a good idea, it is not essential. There have been several times in my life I have simply used pencil and paper to record what I was doing because I didn't have a mala, so don't feel inhibited about starting if you don't have one. As long as your Will is there, you can accomplish working with mantras. An advanced technique of tracking repetitions of mantras only requires your fingers even, so all one truly has to do is learn mantras and get to work.

Originating from other spiritual systems are parallel concepts that could best be explained as prayers or affirmations, or hybrids of both. They accomplish a goal similar to what was discussed earlier about affirmations, but have more of a chant format to them, and have a spiritual bent and emphasis. Many people mistakenly call them mantras, but they are technically not. And even functionally they are different in that they are more hypnotic in nature whereas mantras are more energy body manipulative, but the two techniques usually share the same end result, so they fall into the same category.

Banishing Rituals of the Pentagrams and Hexagrams

We'll end this chapter by discussing my favorite set of rituals in the Western Esoteric Tradition, especially considering they can be used for a variety of purposes including protection, making them some of the most flexible rituals available. They are also some of the most popular rituals, and because of that, they have been written about extensively, so there is no shortage of material available. I want to take time to discuss them now, because it has been my experience that they are the most potent forms of banishing rituals I have encountered. I have seen disciplined routines of their execution completely turn lives around for the positive time and again. I have seen them at work in my life as well. However, they take time to work, so they require discipline and patience.

These rituals derive from the practices of The Hermetic Order of the Golden Dawn and its tradition. They are similar to mantras in that they are spiritual technology and can be used in a modular fashion. Or, they can be used in their pure form in line with the practices of the Golden Dawn. The rituals are different from mantras in that while you are vibrating certain notes and tones, you are also tracing either pentagrams or hexagrams in the air, and third, visualizing particular images and invoking certain forces. Yes, they are advanced, but what they deliver is on a level unparalleled.

I like to include them in all discussions concerned with psychic protection because when people ask me what the 'big guns' are, this is always the answer.

This chapter provides a brief overview that hits on a variety of general subjects and points concerned with

Psychic Protection

psychic protection. It is meant as an introduction to encourage you to answer the questions posed here as to how you can protect yourself from a spiritual perspective. Take from this what you will, leave what you choose, but know that if you are dealing with mental plane attacks, rising to the spiritual is the next logical step.

Chapter Ten
Living Spirituality

To round this book out, we will change our focus to look at the ultimate psychic protection: focused growth. I dare tread into sketchy ground here and will share cursory thoughts on spirituality in general. I say this is sketchy ground because your spiritual path is unique to you, so by and large, my thoughts are from the outside, and not from the perspective of someone living it. However, there are key points, common to most people, that can be addressed to assist in your development.

If you are truly focused on the development of the self and your spirituality, you continually evolve and spirituality mature, making it harder for malevolent beings to negatively impact you – the desired result of this book.

Expanding upon something I mentioned earlier, energy goes where attention flows, meaning that if we are focused on a singularity, the impact of polarity situations does not affect us in the same way or with the same intensity as it does others. This does have an impact on our morality and ethics, which we should note and address periodically.

The singularity is our personal development and spiritual growth. Why do I differentiate between the two? Other authors might emphasize one or the other, or treat them as one in the same, but they are very different. How do I know this? Why am I confident in that statement? Well, language is the reason. We're going to break this down for further insight that can be applied to your work. Let's first look at the spiritual side of things. After all, thought begets form.

Spirituality

Interestingly enough, the older I get, the more I see this word needs further clarification and explanation, because a lot of people think it means something other than it does. Being a spiritual person is in no way indicative of one's character! Just because someone is a spiritual person, this does not necessarily equate with having a moral high ground. Being a spiritual person simply means that you work with the spiritual side of life, or some could say, the unseen forces of the cosmos. That's it, nothing more, nothing less. There seems to be a lot of confusion and misunderstanding about this in the world today, so this is my attempt to clarify the matter. For example, demons are just as spiritual as angels, so you have to be specific.

Part of the understanding lies in when and how this idea came into being. In the early part of the 21st century, more and more people were declaring themselves "spiritual but not religious." They got this idea from writings that occurred in the 1960's e.v. (Era Vulgaris). The idea discussed here is that one can be a spiritually minded and focused person without submitting to any outside authoritarian structure, particularly a religion. In other words, you can develop a deep, rich, meaningful inner life, without the restrictions that come with a religion.

We see, then, that in this context, the word "spiritual" is used as synonymous with being someone who constantly works constantly on their enlightenment. Historically, this is true, and the two words have been used interchangeably, so I can understand where all of this is coming from, I get it. But we are no longer in the 20th century, so it is time to update our understanding of all of these concepts. Let's start with the word spiritual.

The word spiritual conveys a concept, which is that there is a focus on the spiritual world, the world of the spirit. Astral plane, etheric plane, whatever term you want to use, is what is being discussed here. Thus, someone who is a spiritual person makes it a point to work with these energies in hopefully healthy ways for their greatest growth and good, and the greatest growth and good of those around them. We cannot assume, though, that they will achieve this. There is a wide spectrum of people currently manifested into physical reality, and they come from all levels of vibration. What this means is that just because someone calls themselves spiritual, does not necessarily mean they are an ethical person. I really wish I didn't have to write this but feel I must. I have known my share of frauds, phonies, and other dubious types over the last twenty years or so, which is why I share this here, as the final piece of psychic protection. Saying you are "spiritual but not religious," is about the same as saying you are "Christian" or "Muslim." We will come back to this later in the text for clarification. Well, to me, it means about the same, really. I believe spirituality indicates focus and attention, that's all.

The reason this is important when it comes to psychic protection is that if you're not careful, you may subconsciously put someone on a pedestal when they say they are spiritual, and many times this leads to sorrow down the road. This is called the assumption of authority, which works in a few ways. First, this is a technique many occult authors use to try and give more credence to their work. This isn't as common now as it used to be, but many in occultism still do it. For example, if you were going to write an occult book and you wanted people to give it more weight and credence than other books, you could assume the non de plume of "Hermes," or some other figure that people know and respect. Look at it this way. Which sounds better, a book written by "Bob" who is a new author, or "Hermes," who has a long-standing and respectable reputation? The other way the assumption of authority works is that many times we subconsciously put some people in our lives on a mental pedestal as a voice of authority on a particular subject. The latter is what ties into the book here. Just because someone is well known as an authority on 'X' (name a subject), doesn't mean they have any more of a moral code than you or anyone else, for that matter. It took me a long time to train that trait out of my mind, so I can relate if it takes you a while to process this and adapt, but it is worth it. The only danger you risk when you do this is that if you're not careful, you may become cynical in the process, which is not always a good thing.

Technically, almost everyone is spiritual, even atheists, if they are familiar with science, at least, because more and more scientific evidence is showing that there is a vast, invisible side to nature and reality, so to deny its existence is true denial. Recent scientific exploration is even addressing what happens to our consciousness when we die. While this is inconclusive at this point, it is still worth keeping in mind because it tells us that occultism and science are healing a centuries old rift, but in new, more scientific and less faith-based ways. So, spirituality in the sense we are discussing it here, is part of the nature of reality, and is thus a scientific subject in a lot of ways, or you can at least apply scientific methods and principles when exploring it. Keep all of this in mind throughout your day to day life so that you don't accidentally put someone on a pedestal in your mind, which could cause you to turn a blind eye to red flags that would normally protect you.

Living Your Spiritual Truth

Now that we have established a clear and working definition of spirituality, let's discuss what it means to live it. This is something I was introduced to a few years ago through astrology, and have not only found it useful since then, but also something that other people connect with, which is the ability to live your spiritual truth. This takes your personal development to the next level. It's an easy lesson: walk your talk. While this may seem like a no brainer, to many people it is not, and can therefore be something to improve in order to improve your personal development and protect your energy. After all, as I mentioned earlier, there is something to the idea of purity of focus, especially as it applies to protection.

There is an easy way to approach this, but doing it is another story, because in the short term it will take a lot of mental energy and discipline. In short, practice what you preach, and do what you say. The marriage of your spiritual values to the physical world we live in can be a little tricky. Here's an example that I have encountered commonly before. Let's say you believe in being careful with your energy, which includes protecting it, and also being careful who you spend your time with. This means, then, that you are careful with your money also, right? After all, money is the physical representation of the exchange of energy, so it stands to reason that someone would be as mindful of that as who they spend their time with. It's just logical. But I think you will know people, as I do, who don't share that belief.

Another example is of someone who claims they believe in oneness, and yet exclude a group of people, or say things like "Except for that person." They always have exceptions to the rule that are thinly veiled beliefs of racism, xenophobia, or any of the other "-isms" out there. So, which is it? Do you believe in oneness or not? If you truly do, then a lot of personal reflection, meditation, and internal work will show you how to believe in oneness and include everyone, yet still be able to be angry at individuals when appropriate. After all, believing in oneness and loving everyone does not mean you are always in a state of love with them! Just ask any parent...

Now we'll look at a third example, but by now I'm sure you get the point and can think of your own examples from your own experiences and life. A third example would be someone who makes bold claims to be very spiritually advanced and powerful, yet constantly has a drama in their life, and they show no signs of having stability in the world. This is someone who does probably know their material, but they have not learned how to apply what they have learned to provide for their needs. The key thing to remember is the criteria by which you judge. Each person has their own lifestyle, so it is hard to judge someone if you haven't walked a mile in their shoes. To one person, success in life means standing on one's own feet, but to another, it may be living with an elderly person to take care of them, sacrificing certain things for something greater. With astute observation, it will become clear where particular individuals fall in this spectrum.

Judge Not... Ha!

While not directly related to psychic protection, it is a discernment skill that can be used to protect your energy, by remembering it is a tool in your spiritual arsenal. Being non-judgmental is a common tactic many will use to save face from saying something risqué. Eventually, this becomes habit, and subconsciously they turn into what they were initially fighting against becoming. I have known many people through the years who use the phrase "I'm not judging, but..." as a tool of emotional manipulation. A related way this phrase (I'm not judging) is to use it as a cop out so as to avoid making a decision or taking a stance. Like every other subject we've been discussing here, there is a sliding scale of grey to be looked at when you're dealing with this, so let's break things down for clarity.

Commonly, people do their best not to judge because they don't want their lower ego to get the best of them, so in this way it is used as a protective measure. I completely agree with this motivation, and I fully encourage it! But something else should be taken into consideration.

This phrase is inspired by a quote from the Christian Bible: "Judge not, that ye be not judged. For with what judgment ye judge, ye shall be judged, and with what measure ye mete, it shall be measured to you again." (Matthew 7:1-2, King James Version). In other words, as it is commonly said, "Judge not, lest ye be judged yourself. By the measure you judge, you too, will be judged." (Me!) There is much spiritual wisdom contained in that phrase, but usually it is taken out of context.

Essentially, this phrase is saying be careful how severely you judge, because you will be judged just at the same level. It does *not* say you should never judge at all, but rather you should be careful how harshly you judge, because it may come back to you as harshly. It is a lesson in compassion. Too many times people have bastardized this to a shortened version: "Judge not." Wow, talk about missing the point! Judgment is a key discernment skill to develop, but yes, we should be careful to keep our lower ego in check.

After all, you made the judgment call to pick up this book. You make the judgment call every day to get up and do what you need to do. These are choices, and we make judgments with consequences every day of our lives, so to think we shouldn't judge is to not understand decisions, actions, and consequences. It is through judgment that we protect our energy, after all, but we should still practice compassion, sympathy, and empathy *when* we judge.

So yes, we should judge frequently. We should constantly improve our judgment skills, but as we do, we should also exercise forethought and compassion. Now that we have dissected what spiritual is and isn't, let's look at the other side of the equation. Let's take a closer look at religion, because a lot of people are not clear on what religion is, and it is a tricky subject, to be fair.

Religion

Before we discuss a spiritual dimension to this, let's establish a baseline. According to the Oxford Dictionary, the word is defined as "the belief in the existence of a god or gods, and the activities that are connected with the worship of them, or in the teachings of a spiritual leader." The second definition is "One of the systems of faith that are based on the belief in the existence of a particular god or gods, or in the teachings of a spiritual leader." In the name of providing a different perspective, it is worth noting that according to the law of the United States of America, as of the writing of this book, even atheism is classified as a religion. I won't get into the legal jargon here, but feel free to look it up. This means that really, like a lot of words and concepts, there is what is found in the dictionary and through linguistics, and then there is the physical world application of them. And, many times, these two definitions conflict and may not make sense.

Notice how they both include the word god? This shows how narrow the definition of the word is, but also why so many people are adverse to religion. Going by the dictionary definition, the organizations hinted at above are the largest and most well-known, and they all make you believe in a god. A further implication is the dogma that those groups impose in the name of shared beliefs, cohesion, and group power. So, what this means is that for the most part, people have an aversion to dogma and the subjects mentioned above in the definitions. And really, I completely understand that. Heck, I fully support it, actually! The dictionary definitions are too narrow minded and old aeon, and could use some updating, especially when we turn our attention to a third, far different definition.

This enlightened definition comes from Spiritualism and makes much more sense. I always like sharing this because this is the definition that brought me peace of mind when it comes to seeing religion as a positive force, especially during this time of change. In Spiritualism religion is defined as "Living in accord with natural, universal, and spiritual laws." In other words, living in alignment with the world around us. That's a pretty innovative definition, isn't it? It's also light on dogma and widely open to interpretation. What one person considers harmony may not be true for another person, and according to this definition, that is okay and largely healthy.

The way this applies to psychic protection is that it suggests you should do your best, however you define it, to live in line with the world around you. This helps keep the mind and Will focused on your individual needs and what you need to do fulfil them. When you are this focused on your life and spiritual ascent, it is harder for beings, physical or not, to attack you. Through this singularity, you develop a certain type of energetic armor, and it's passive, which means it takes little to no effort to maintain. Oh yeah, speaking of armor...

Shielding and Armor

Many people practice the art of energetic shielding. The way this works is that when they see they are going into a situation where there may be vulnerable to psychic attacks, they prepare themselves mentally and energetically and put up what they call a shield. This is an effective technique, and much has been written about it, especially over the last few years. Shields are generally faith and/or energy based, and almost anyone can create them, because all it requires is mental attention and intent. There is a problem with shielding, though; it can leave you feeling drained because of the amount of energy you expend on it.

Armor, though, is a different story. It is developed in another way, because it can be put on or taken off at a moment's notice. It can also, however, be a permanent protection. It is created through day-to-day energy work over an extended period of time and will remain in effect unless you take it off. I have found that if you develop your armor continuously for a long time, it simply becomes a new state of being. By working with mental armor, you shift your consciousness. Part of this shift is connected with strengthening your Will and also with raising your vibration. Creating and working with mental armor, and the subsequent raising of your vibration, allows you to view situations with more clarity and from new perspectives, which includes more applications of compassion and patience.

You might be wondering how you go about creating mental armor. The answer to that is quite subjective, but there are common traits and characteristics that can be discussed. One of the first things you can do is to make sure you have self-discipline in abundance. If this is already present, the procedure get easier from there. You should also learn some sort of energy movement technique. This can be whatever you want. A lot of people learn the system of Reiki, but there are several other systems out there, and I encourage you to learn at least one so you have a firm understanding of energy and how you may manipulate it. After all, everything is energy. And, think outside the box. A highly effective technique I know is to use symbols to imprint the aura for the sake of protection. This is a very simple and subjective technique, because it only requires two things. First, it requires a knowledge of symbols, as we discussed earlier in the book. When you learn the protective symbols of your chosen pantheon, even if you made that pantheon yourself, then you're ready for step two. This is to focus mentally on imprinting the symbol or symbols onto your aura. This takes only about half an hour each day when you focus and concentrate, mentally visualizing the symbols slowly sinking into a space of about two to three inches away from your physical form, which is where your aura is located. Remember to do this at least twenty-eight days in a row so it gets firmly embedded in your subconscious, although I have noticed that the more you do this, the more you enjoy it, and you generally end up doing it for much longer. This can be quite a fun exercise to keep your imagination active and your focus on your personal and spiritual development. So, if you choose to use this technique, make sure to make this a fun exercise. After all, existence is pure joy, and laughter is the unpronounceable name of god. By making this fun you have already raised your vibration and made your development enjoyable, rather than feeling like it is a chore.

No matter which technique, (shielding or armoring), you use, remember it is going to take discipline and time to cultivate these skills, so be patient. The more patient you are, the stronger your natural defenses will become. This, in turn, means the skills will feel more natural to you, even more so if you stay on course with your development. There is another applicable technique you can use, and while the name of it is occult in nature, millions of people use it every day, regardless of whether or not they are into occultism.

Talismanic Magick

A talisman is an object that is thought to bring good fortune and other beneficent powers to the bearer. If you've ever had a good luck charm, you have been working with this technique. This shows how common a practice it is, yet most people who do it don't look at it that way, but its true none the less. This concept can be expanded to include ideas that are still protective but also unorthodox. The idea that comes to mind here is insurance. It is very common for people across the world to have insurance of some kind, whether it is for a business, a vehicle, health, life, or some other important topic. Insurance is basically something you have

Psychic Protection

so that if an emergency comes up, it can help protect you or at least lessen the impact of whatever event occurs. This is the basic philosophy behind the concept. You have insurance so it is there should you need it, but also because it fulfills the idea that it is better to have it and not need it, so in this way it is something that is acquired in the name of protection. When you look at this from a metaphysical position, it tells you that you are projecting that energy out into the universe. You are being proactive regarding what you are doing. In this way, you tell the universe that you are taking steps to insure success, but are prepared to deal with the outcome if success doesn't manifest. As a matter of fact, the Boy Scouts of America embody this technique in their motto of "always be prepared." During those times when you feel you could use a little extra something to help grease the wheels of your project, this is an easy way to go about it. Best of all, it is completely fluid and flexible.

To Work in Silence

Another proactive protection technique is the idea to work in silence. This is similar to the idea that discretion is the better part of valor. In the Western Esoteric Tradition, this is known as the fourth power of the Sphinx, which is to conceal something, or to work in silence. Not speaking of what you are doing can often be a defensive maneuver in and of itself. The reason for this is that people can send negative energy to you to thwart your efforts, even if that is not their intention. Before we get to that though, let's lay some groundwork. While this might involve some subjectivity, the principles are true almost across the boards.

People send energy to other people almost every moment of the day. This generally occurs when we think about someone, or various situations that elicit an emotional reaction. Each time we think of this, we send a bolt of energy to feed that memory and experience. This is the foundational principle behind the metaphysical teaching "energy follows thought, thought begets form." I wrote about this extensively in *Vocal Magick*, so you can find more information there. However, it is worth coming back to here, because the converse is also true. A lot of the time people are thinking about us too, and when they are, energy is being sent our way. This energy can be either positive or negative, which means that people send out negative energy to other people or situations the more they think about them in a negative way. This can also be extended to include worry energy.

When you or someone you know worries about something, strong, negative energy is sent out to the target. This feeds the strength of the target, and locks both the projector and the target into a polarized relationship, reinforcing the relationship with the duality existence we all experience while in physical form. This means that we are all exposed to negative energies that are out of our control all the time. Much like the fact we are all exposed to cosmic radiation every day yet don't suffer the effects, we are constantly a receiver and a sponge. Granted, the people who project worried energy generally approach life from a fear based (read: weak) perspective, but many times, in their minds, they feel they are doing the right thing. This is especially true of those who engage in a lot of prayers. We can't hold ill-will towards them, because their intent is founded in love. Remember the key piece of information here, though: *They only worry about what they know about!*

Sometimes it is helpful to keep your meaningful personal development projects to yourself while working on them, so that others cannot accidentally send you negative energy through worrying about your success. This also keeps the information away from detractors, too. While many people might want to see you succeed, there

Psychic Protection

could be just as many who want to see you fail. But they only get the information you allow them to have. Thus, you can appreciate the protective skill of operating in silence.

By concealing what you are doing, you are in effect protecting yourself from the ill intentions of others. However, you might also be concerned that you're not putting yourself in a position to receive supportive energy from loved ones. Therefore, it is okay to tell trusted loved ones who you're sure wish you no ill intent but listen to your intuition. In any event, I'm sure the point is made that you can tell someone if you choose but be mindful of this principle. Obfuscation can also result in what is known as a *sin of omission*. This is when you intentionally leave something important out, and what you left out could change the whole tone of the experience. Keeping one's mouth shut is one of the best skills you can cultivate through your development.

Practicing the art of discretion through such practices as a "need to know" basis, and "plausible deniability," we protect ourselves from the negative energy of others, even if their intention is well-meaning, and through doing this, we raise our vibration by showing the universe that we are selective when it comes to what we are doing. "Never cast your pearls before swine" also comes to mind, as does "why give someone steak if they have a taste for hamburger?" A general rule of thumb to abide by is that not everything we do should be the business of others. To remember this is to put your spirituality into practice. As my friend Bob North said, if we are the microcosm of the universal macrocosm, and it is half concealed, then perhaps we should be, too.

Working with this principle will take time, and you may adjust it to your spiritual path as you see fit, but through extended work you will find the right balance of silence vs speech, which will further strengthen your mental armor.

Bill Duvendack

There is Love, and There is Love

Finally, we come to the end of this chapter and almost the book for that matter. We will wrap things up on a high note, focusing on the power of love. It may not seem like it fits here, but there is a lot of powerful energy that love can provide us in the name of our spiritual connection and personal growth. There are a few things I would like to focus on that can be of use when it comes to protecting your energy from a space of love. First, we must understand what love is in a clear and metaphysical way. In other words, in a way that we can apply to everyday life. This makes it practical love, if you will.

The Ancient Greeks had six different words for love, yet they knew that all forms of love are equally valid. Some of these can be used to protect your energy, but to do so may require looking at situations in a new way and from a new perspective. We will now take a closer look at the different forms of love and discuss the protective properties they contain.

The six types of love are:

1) Eros, which is sexual love, commonly known as passion

2) Philia, which is the type of love that comes with a deep friendship

3) Ludus, which is defined as playful love

4) Agape love, which is love for everyone, which could include unconditional love

5) Pragma, which is longstanding love

6) Philautia, which is the love of the self.

It is obvious how certain of these types of love might offer protective qualities. For example, philia. This type of love can provide an ally on one's side no matter what, so you know you don't have to face most things in life alone or be caught off guard. Another example of a protective quality of love can be found in philautia, the love of the self. After all, if you don't

Psychic Protection

love yourself first, how can you love anyone else? And, part of loving yourself is taking proactive steps to raise your vibration and protect your energy.

Really, you could easily find protective qualities and traits in all of these kinds of love, and I encourage you to do so as a mind and spirit building exercise. Often, people think of love outside the realm of psychic protection, but it should definitely be part of the conversation. Love is a high vibration, after all, and we should always be looking at the mental high ground, as I mentioned earlier. This includes the metaphysical idea of raising your vibration beyond a polarity existence.

We live in a polarity-based reality, as has been proven by science dating back to Isaac Newton and his third law, which effectively states that if something is true, so is its opposite. Almost two thousand years before him, Hermeticism said the same in its axiom: "As above, so below, as within, so without." There's no denying this fact of the physical world, but it is predominantly restricted to this plane.

There is a trick to working with this, though, which is that we live in a polarity-based reality, so technically, while we're in physical form, there is no getting away from it. As a matter of fact, friction from polar opposites can release a lot of energy that can be applied to the projects of your Will. This doesn't mean you shouldn't strive to go beyond it, though, but a lot of this entails a shift in consciousness more than how you interact with the outside world. Rising above polarity is a mental activity that can be quite useful, but most of the work is internal. It concerns seeing situations from an inclusive perspective, rather than a dual one. I have found this very useful when it comes to the decision-making process. Looking for solutions that entail everyone and everything in an inclusive way is a challenge, for sure, but is worth the mental work. For example, when you look at the division in the world today, you can either see the division, which is very real, or you can mentally step back and look at the bigger picture. What is causing the division? How can solutions that take care of everyone be found? Why do people approach problems from an "either or" perspective? Why can't it be both?

As you can see from these examples, they are tough questions that require new ways of thinking, and courage to take chances and act on them. This is a hidden lesson of psychic protection – courage and taking chances. If we are under psychic attack or mental manipulation for extended periods of time, we might default mentally to a safe head space. In psychology, this is known as having a bunker mentality. This phrase is borrowed from the military and is based on the idea that when things get intense, you should lower your head and dig down in the bunker until the danger passes. I point this out because many people approach life from a bunker mentality by default. This is something that occurs over time, and usually happens subconsciously, so many are not aware they are doing it. The bunker mentality might have its uses, but if it becomes a long-standing habit it begins to infect the consciousness in a negative way, limiting the enjoyment of life and acting as a barrier to the spiritual lessons we came down here to learn. Courage is the way to proceed, but this is not an absolute either, as sometimes applied courage without forethought is a recipe for disaster. All of this simply reminds us of the value of periodic internal review and seeking new ways to grow. In this way, it is the most powerful psychic protection. By staying on target when it comes to your personal growth, and being mindful of finding your middle point of courage vs using the tried and true methods, you will maintain proactivity, and in so doing, your vibration will remain in a state of positive flux that makes it harder for energy leaks and leeches to lock onto us. As has been said many times in professional sports, "The best defense is a good offense."

Afterword

As you can see by now, the secret to psychic protection lies in the mind and the ability to apply the principles we have discussed in practical ways. That's it, nothing more. It's not as scary as you may think to be under a psychic attack because it's not as daunting as you might believe to protect yourself. After all, people protect themselves unknowingly all the time, so it's not really that big of a deal; it's easier to protect yourself than you may think. Boundaries, responsibilities, and maturity are all proactive ways to make sure you are safe when living life.

True psychic attacks require several moving parts to be a legitimate attack. First, you have to have people in your life who have the desire and means to attack you. This rules out the bulk of people in society today, because it does take true occult skills to pull off a psychic attack. An easy way to think about this is to take a mental tally as to whether or not you have people in your life who practice the more of occult spiritual traditions, such as witchcraft, Voodoo, etc. Secondly, they also require your belief in polarity consciousness. After all, the best revenge against someone who wishes you failure is success and living life to the fullest. Some could argue that this is emphasis on denial, but it does not have to develop into that if you are aware of the trap and focus on avoiding it. Third, you have to believe you can be attacked. Yes, some attacks can be successful even if you don't believe such attacks are possible, but that is another matter entirely for another time. There are many times in my life when I have been psychically attacked, and the attacks didn't work because I gave them no mental time or effort. I turned a blind eye to them, and it was enough to nullify the effects that were aimed at me because I didn't feed energy into them. But there have also been times when I was psychically attacked and suffered tangible effects. The difference was that the successful attacks came from certain kinds of occult traditions that are not commonly known about or practiced, and to explain the details would take a book in and of itself to explain.

If you are not surrounded by people who practice those occult traditions, then the probability of being attacked immediately decreases. You may still be surrounded by psychic and energy vampires, and some of them may not be aware of what they're doing, but if this is the case, then you have to handle it with care. Now you have the tools to combat attacks and succeed.

Keep in mind that this is an overview and a beginner's book to the principles behind psychic protection, and as is true so many times, someone who came before me summarized it succinctly. These words of wisdom should be kept in mind regarding all things in life. To quote Dion Fortune from her book *Psychic Self-Defense*: "Times, points of view and fashions change, but never principles."

Bibliography For Further Reading

Ask the Right Questions by Debbie Ford
Crystal Power, Crystal Healing by Michael Gienger
Crystal Prescriptions Book 5: Space Clearing, Feng Shui and Psychic Protection, by Judy Hall
Cunningham's Encyclopedia of Crystal, Gem, & Metal Magic by Scott Cunningham
Cunningham's Encyclopedia of Magical Herbs by Scott Cunningham
Compendium of Herbal Magick by Paul Beyerl
Healing Mantras by Thomas Ashley-Farrand
Magical Housekeeping by Tess Whitehurst
Psychic Self Defense by Dion Fortune
Sacred Space by Denise Linn
The Art of Psychic Protection by Judy Hall
The Magical Household by Scott Cunningham
The Magical and Ritual Use of Herbs by Richard Alan Miller
The Master Book of Herbalism by Paul Beyerl
The Naked Ape: A Zoologist's Study of the Human Animal by Desmond Morris
The Witch's Shield: Protection Magic and Self-Defense by Christopher Penczak
Your Life: Why It Is the Way It Is and What You Can Do About It by Bruce McArthur

*And, don't forget what we discussed throughout the book. Almost every spiritual tradition has specific material on protection, so consult those sources when appropriate.

About the Author

Bill Duvendack is an ordained independent Spiritualist minister who is an internationally known psychic, presenter, and author. He has presented in many venues, ranging from colleges and high schools to national and international conferences. He is the author of eleven published books, including *Vocal Magick*, *The Metaphysics of Magick*, and *In the Shadow of the Watchtower, Enochian Grimoire Volume 1*, *Spirit Relations*, and *Dark Fruit, Enochian Grimoire Volume 2*. He has had over a dozen essays published in various anthologies, and his magical writings have been translated into 6 languages. He regularly teaches classes on magick, astrology, and modern spirituality nationally and via webinars. He has been interviewed by the NY Times, RTE 1, and has made many TV and radio appearances. For more information about him, please consult his website: www.418ascendant.com.

Other Books by Bill Duvendack

Spirit Relations
Vocal Magick
The Metaphysics of Magick
Astrology in Theory & Practice
In the Shadow of the Watchtower: Enochian Grimoire
Volume One
Dark Fruit: Enochian Grimoire Volume Two
A Draconian Egyptian Grimoire
Sat En Anpu: a Book of Anubis
Awakening Lucifer (with Asenath Mason)
Qliphothic Astrology
Oraculum Leviathan Tarot Set (with Asenath Mason)

More Bill Duvendack from Immanion Press

 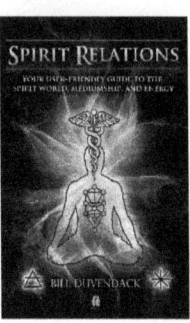

Vocal Magick
Through exercising control over your language and speech, you can create many powerfully profound changes in your consciousness. By understanding how to accomplish these changes, you can put yourself in a position to be more in control of yourself and your life. Within this book, you will look at applications, universal laws, and address the use of subtleties. This will open the door to profound shifts in not only how you view reality, but also what you can do about it! ISBN: 978-1-905713-99-8 Price: £10.99, $16.99, €15.50

Spirit Relations
Are you looking for a book that teaches you mediumship, rather than merely sharing an individual's stories of their own work? Are you tired of the dogma that is erroneously attached to this unique skill? Do you want a book with exercises to help you develop your psychic abilities in a more hands-on fashion? Look no further, because all this and more is covered in *Spirit Relations*. Written by a professional medium, this book not only covers channeling, but also discusses the energetic body of a person, and what to expect when you begin to interact with spirits on a regular basis. ISBN: 978-0995511-75-0 Price: £10.99, $16.99, €3.99

www.immanion-press.com

Recent Titles from Megalithica Books

Coming Forth by Day by Storm Constantine

This book explores the myths of Ancient Egyptian gods and goddesses – showing how their stories relate to aspects of our lives, hopes and aspirations, and how we can learn from these ancient narratives. Through 28 deep and evocative pathworkings and rituals, the author provides a rich and vivid system of magic that the practitioner – whether experienced or a novice – can utilize in the search for self-knowledge, and to help themselves, others and the world around them. ISBN: 978-1-912241-11-8 Price: £12.99, $16.99

SHE: Primal Meetings with the Dark Goddess by Storm Constantine & Andrew Collins

The Dark Goddess is unpredictable, dispassionate, cruel, and often deadly. She reflects our deepest desires, fears, hopes and expectations. In this fully-illustrated book, Storm Constantine and Andrew Collins have selected a fascinating range of 34 goddesses, including some who are not so well-known. The pathworkings to meet them and explore their realms will offer insight into these often-misunderstood deities. (This title is also available as a limited edition, numbered hardback.) ISBN: 978-1-912241-06-4 Price: £12.99, $18.99

My First Book of Magic by Dolores Ashcroft-Nowicki

I want to tell you how the Pagan Way works, what it does, and how it makes you feel. I want you to know the joy this oldest of all traditions can bring you. The way of sharing it with humans, elementals, sprites, animals, plants, trees, and of course other pagans.

If you have a child in your life that has the look of far memory in their eyes, gift them with this guide. If you remember the child you were, read this book and reopen the gates of your wonder." – Ivo Dominguez Jr., author of 'Keys to Perception'.

ISBN: 978-1-912241-10-1 Price: £10.99, $15.99

www.immanion-press.com

Egyptian-Themed Magic From Megalithica Books

Sekhem Heka by Storm Constantine

Drawing upon her experiences in Egyptian Magic and the energy healing systems of Reiki and Seichim, Storm Constantine developed this new system for practitioners of both magic and energy healing. Incorporating ritual and visualisation into a progressive journey through the seven energy centres of the body, Sekhem Heka can be practiced by those who are already attuned to an energy healing modality, as well as those who are simply interested in the magical aspects of the system. Sekhem Heka is designed to help the practitioner work upon self-evolution. Each of the seven tiers focuses upon a particular Ancient Egyptian god or goddess, including practical exercises and rites. ISBN pbk: 9781905713134, £12.99 $21.99

Graeco-Egyptian Magic by Tony Mierzwicki

This book outlines a daily practice involving planetary Hermeticism, drawn from the original texts and converted into a format that fits easily into the modern magician's practice. As a magickal system, Graeco-Egyptian magick represents the last flowering of paganism before it was wiped out by the Christian juggernaut. It is a hybrid system that blended ancient Sumerian and Egyptian magick with the relatively more modern Greek and Judaic systems. ISBN pbk: 9781912241033, £12.99 $21.99

The Travellers' Guide to the Duat by Kiya Nicoll

Planning a trip to the Egyptian spirit world? Like any responsible traveller, you want to know something about the history, geography, and politics of your destination. You want to know what documents you need to have in order for customs and immigration, what precautions to take, how to book a boat tour, where to stay, what to eat, and when you'll get the most interesting sightseeing opportunities. Laced through its humorous presentation you will find extensive information about ancient Egyptian religion and magical practice. Renditions of ancient spells in modern poetry mark each section, showing the ancient magical texts in a new light. The Beautiful West awaits! Book your tour today!
ISBN pbk: 9781905713738, $19.99, £10.99

www.immanion-press.com

www.ingramcontent.com/pod-product-compliance
Lightning Source LLC
LaVergne TN
LVHW090115080426
835507LV00040B/889

Praise for *Success Proof*

"Jason's stark honesty about his struggles with church leadership and with his own faith struggles is refreshing in a sea of books filled with pandering and empty platitudes. God continually shows us, again and again, that He uses the broken and wounded to point us back to Him. Jason bravely bears his own deep wound as a beacon back to the heart of God."
~**Dan Foote**, *Men's Community Pastor at Flatirons Community Church in Lafayette, CO*

"As a pastor's daughter, I fully appreciate Hanselman's honest insight into the humanity of ministry. Success Proof is as thought-provoking as it is entertaining."
~ **Angela Strong**, *Award Winning Author*

Jason Hanselman is one of the most honest, creative and original thinkers of our time. A thousand years from now, people will read his books and say: "Wow! That was the guy who finally got it right."
~**John C. Drew, Ph.D.**, *Managing Director, Drew & Associates*